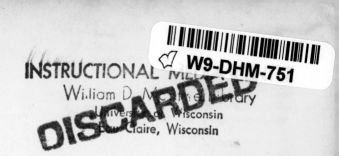

Mickey Mantle

OF THE YANKEES

Mickey Mantle

OF THE YANKEES

by Gene Schoor

NEW YORK G. P. Putnam's Sons

Library of Congess Catalog Card
Number 58-13314
MANUFACTURED IN THE UNITED STATES OF AMERICA
BY THE COLONIAL PRESS INC., CLINTON, MASS.

To
FRAN—

Who can hit from either side of the plate

Mickey Mantle

OF THE YANKEES

I.

THE reporters clustered around Joe DiMaggio in the Yankee training camp in the spring of 1951 like bees around honey. Jolting Joe was not only the big man in the camp, he was the biggest man in baseball. What Joe said was what the fans back home wanted to read and mull over.

"Another big year coming up for you, Joe?" one of the reporters asked.

Joe's famous poker face broke into a grin. "If I have another one like last year, I'll die a happy man."

The reporters didn't need to be told what he was talking about. In 1949 he had undergone an operation on an ailing heel. He had been out for most of the season. Then, when most fans had counted him out, he had come back. In '50 he had belted thirty-two home runs and had almost singlehandedly slammed the Yanks home to their second world championship in a row.

"The fans are not worrying about you dying, Joe. Bad heels or not, you're built like a mountain. But they want to know about the year coming up."

"I think it'll be all right," said Joe thoughtfully. "I'm not kidding myself. I can't keep playing forever.

9

I'm not a kid any more. But I think I got one good season left, maybe two. I've been a long time in the game."

After that, like a bunch of nice old ladies at a family reunion, the reporters rehashed baseball history for nearly an hour.

And then, right in the middle of the conversation, new history began to be made.

Crack!

The reporters' heads jerked around just in time to see the ball jet its way over a chicken-wire fence.

"Holy cow!" one of them said.

"That one went four hundred feet if it went a foot," said Joe after seeing the ball come down.

Then they all turned in the direction of home plate.

"Don't tell me that kid there belted it!" said a reporter.

"It sure looks like it," Joe answered, chuckling. "Casey has a heck of a lot of good kids to work with this year. Three or four of the rookies look like they might even make it back to New York with us."

"What's *that* kid's name?"

"Mantle. Mickey Mantle. Real nice kid, too."

"A lucky wallop," one hard-boiled reporter said. "The kid'll probably go through life wondering how he ever knocked that one out of the park."

The game they were watching was a practice session. The two sides had been chosen from within the Yankee ranks. After Mantle's blow, it became dull again. So the marathon interview with DiMaggio resumed.

"Mantle's coming up again," said Joe, after a while. "Watch the kid swing."

Mantle stood calmly at the plate. He was big across the shoulders, with powerful wrists and big hands, and he stroked the big bat smoothly yet powerfully at each offering. He didn't fidget. He just stood there, legs wide apart, swinging his big bat back and forth.

The rookie pitcher on the mound looked down at Mantle, toed the pitching rubber, then came in with a blazing fast ball. Mantle strode forward eager to meet the pitch and whipped his big bat savagely into the ball.

It was a vicious drive that took off over the outstretched hands of the shortstop, who had leaped high into the air. The ball continued on and out over the head of the hard-running center fielder until it disappeared over the deep reaches of the center-field wall.

"What do you know," said Joe, scratching his head. "Hitting long ones is a habit with the kid. He looks real good to me. How does he look to you fellows?"

The newspapermen, who had gulped as if there were only one Adam's apple among them, stood there gaping. "Boy!" said one of them. "You didn't even have to see that one. All you had to do was listen. What a shot! That kid's all muscle!"

"Hey, Casey!" yelled one of the scribes to the Yankee manager who was a dozen feet away. "Fill us in on the young DiMaggio."

Casey Stengel did a little dance as he came over. "Friends, it's dancin' weather we got today! What a sweetheart of a day!"

"Casey, whenever one of your players belts one out of park, you think it's good weather. You wouldn't care if it was snowing. Give us a little background on Mantle."

"He was down in Joplin last year," said the Old Professor. "He comes from poor minin' people and he ain't any more anxious to work in a regular job than you fellas. So he played shortstop. Pretty bad, too. Year before that he idled away half a season with Independence. That's Class D ball. Just before that, he claims, he was in high school learnin' his R's. He's just a little schoolboy, still learnin'."

"That's all the experience he has?"

"How much did you have when you was nineteen?"

"He's great!"

"Maybe he's got it in him to be a player and maybe he ain't." Casey's smile lit up his face. "I'm way ahead of you fellas. I know what you've been sayin'." Then he started to imitate the hard-boiled reporter's voice. "Old Casey got the luck. Came to the Yanks in '49. DiMag starts limpin'. So Tommy Henrich starts battin' like DiMag and makes Old Casey look good. Then, a year later, DiMag makes a great comeback and Casey's got another pennant. This year the Old Professor's dead. Dead as a dodo. That's what you say. And, to make sure, you'd like to load me up with raw rookies runnin' away from regular work!"

"Casey," said the reporter, "you're off your bean."

"Man off his bean don't win two series in a row," said Casey, his eyes glistening. Then he danced himself away.

As the days went by in the camp at Phoenix, the reporters' attention was concentrated more and more on Mickey Mantle. He was the greenest rookie there, but he was belting the ball like an all-time master. To make things more confusing, he was the shyest rookie the team or the scribes had ever seen.

"What is this with you," sports editor Max Kase asked him one day, "an act or something? Rookies who get a single now and then are walking around crowing all over the place. There's never a peep out of you. I don't think you've talked ten sentences since you've been up here."

"Well, sir," said Mantle, who confounded the camp by calling everyone *sir,* "I'm just working hard on doing my best. I think Mr. Casey doesn't think it's good enough. I just keep hoping that I can make it with one of the farm clubs. I sure would love to play with the Yankees some day. I just hope I can."

The fantastic thing was that he seemed to believe what he was saying. Everyone was impressed with Mantle except Mantle!

The feature stories that began to be wired and mailed out about Mantle were amazing. Right from the start, the writers began talking about him in terms of his being another DiMaggio. Not just a good player. Not merely a potential wearer of the Yankee uniform. But another DiMaggio! All on the basis of a few practice games at a training camp!

Whatever goes up high gets shot at. And Mantle soon found that he was no exception. Many of the reporters had praised him so lavishly that their own feature stories worried them. They started to have second thoughts about Mantle. And then a "scientific" explanation about Mantle was born.

"The air in Phoenix," his critics would say, "is thin. A ball travels a lot faster and farther here than it does elsewhere."

This view began to catch on. But then Casey, who had held his peace, brought the critics down with one whiplash of his famous tongue.

"That's enough of this bunk," he said. "We're all breathing the same 'thin air' around here, but I don't see nobody but Mantle losin' all the balls over the fence for us."

"We'll see how he does against pros in the exhibition games," some of the die-hard skeptics answered. "After all, these are just kidding-around games we've seen here. The teams are full of rookies, and pros who aren't straining themselves while limbering up. We'll see how great Mantle is when he faces real big-leaguers."

The skeptics didn't have to wait long. On the exhibition tour Mickey looked even better than in camp! His fielding was ordinary. As a matter of fact, his fielding was just that of an average shortstop in the minor leagues. The outfield was new to him and he was completely at sea during those first few weeks. But everything else he showed was top-drawer stuff. He ran like a rabbit on a target range. His arm was as powerful as his powerhouse of a body and he threw straight as an arrow. But his hitting astounded everyone—even the skeptical reporters. A switch-hitter who could belt them out into upper space batting right- or left-handed!

Overnight, the glare of publicity began to move from DiMaggio to a kid named Mantle! The sportswriters in the camp went wild over him!

The whole Yankee team pronounced him to be one of baseball's coming stars.

Joe DiMaggio made the blood of all baseball fans race faster by publicly saying that he saw no reason why Mantle shouldn't be able to step into his shoes in a pretty short time!

White Sox General Manager Frank Lane, who had heard quite correctly that the Yanks had signed Mantle without a fabulous amount of bonus money, told the press: "And to think they got him for nothing! Nothing—do you hear? Why, for a prospect like that, I'd bury him in thousand-dollar bills."

How many thousand-dollar bills? the press wanted to know. Lane's startling answer was that he would have been prepared to pay as high as a *quarter of a million dollars* just for the privilege of signing the young rookie!

The question that was suddenly on everyone's lips was whether this green kid would start the season with the Yanks. Could he make the jump from nowhere to the world champion Yankees overnight? Would Mantle have the stuff to stick with the greatest stars in all of baseball?

But the man who had to make the decision wasn't talking. Or, rather, Old Casey was talking too much. Battle-wise in the ways of the press, he was expertly drowning his questioners in words. One remark would convince the scribes that the answer was Yes, and the next one would sound like No.

"That kid Mantle," said Casey, "is one of the greatest natural ball players these eyes ever watched. He got a great chance to stay right up there with us."

Then Mantle would put on a Yank uniform?

"Well, I ain't sure he's ready. Right this here minute he ain't no big-league outfielder. Will I keep him in my pocket and take him home with me? Will I send him down to some farm to drink a little more milk and get more sunburned—how the heck should I know?"

Casey wasn't just trying to outfox the press. There was a struggle going on within him that none of the outsiders knew about, and he didn't care to talk about it. But to his coaches, Bill Dickey and Jim Turner, he spoke his mind.

"I just can't get Old John McGraw out of my head. I been walkin' around and thinkin' about him all day long. The thing's gettin' so bad, I been dreamin' about the old boy!"

The late John McGraw had not only been the fabulous manager of the Giants during their great championship days, but he had also been Casey's manager when Casey was a young ballplayer. Casey idolized McGraw.

"I keep rememberin' how Old John kept little Melvin Ott right by him, like a momma hen takin' care of a little chick. And Ott, you'll keep in mind, was just a wee lad of sixteen when he first found his way to the Polo Grounds."

The problem that was gripping Casey was this: When was the right time to bring up to the majors a rookie who showed promise of greatness? Right away, as McGraw had done with Ott? Or later, after he had been thoroughly seasoned in the minors? Bring him up too fast and you take a chance on ruining him for good. Casey knew that as well as anyone.

There had never been any doubt in Casey's mind about what he had in Mantle. But his delight didn't answer for him the question of whether Mickey was yet ready for the big leagues.

Stay with him? Or send him down to Binghamton or Kansas City for more experience? The problem was beginning to make Old Casey lose sleep.

But what did Mantle think about all this?

One afternoon, sitting in the locker room and drinking milk from a wax container, the young rookie told the other players how he felt:

"I won't make it this year. I know that. There are so many things I have to learn it'll take me a couple of years at least. Maybe a lot longer. I'm no DiMaggio at bat or in the field. I hope they send me to Kansas City. I got a lot to learn, and I sure hope they play me every day. That's the only way to learn big-league baseball— by playing every day."

The team had come to respect the youngster's modesty. And so had the press. It was not a pose. He was like that all the time. He almost never spoke until he was spoken to. And then he would answer simply and honestly.

As the exhibition games came to an end, the publicity shifted completely from DiMaggio to Mantle. The dispatches that went out to the papers were sheer raves. The greatest baseball reporters cheered Mantle as if with one voice. A story filed by sportswriter Arch Murray to the *New York Post* in that hectic preseason period was typical:

> Mantle has been a sensation since the day he hit camp, but he increases in stature almost every day. The way he continues to pound the ball . . . and his incredible speed make your eyes pop.

And then the big story exploded all over the sports pages.

With the exhibition games over, the fellows who tote up the averages found that Mantle had led the entire Yankee team!

His over-all batting average in the exhibition games had been a fantastic .402!

Then came Casey's formal announcement about the fate of the rookies: Starting the season with the Yanks would be Gil McDougald, an agile infielder, and Tom Morgan, a promising hurler.

What about Mantle?

Casey smiled a Cheshire-cat smile. Then he said, "You don't think Old Casey lost all his marbles yet, do you? Sure, I'm taking the kid back home with us. He's liable to be in the opening game at Yankee Stadium."

Mantle had made it!

The young kid shortstop from Joplin, the small-town boy who had played high-school baseball just two years before, would wear the famous Yankee uniform. Never before in all its long and glorious history had a high-school player from a Class D team made the Big Jump to the Bombers overnight! But Mickey Mantle, Mutt Mantle's kid, from Commerce, Oklahoma, had done it.

Mantle was by now a household name to every baseball fan in America, *and he had never yet played a single big-league game!* It was a Frank Merriwell story come to life!

Could anyone make good under such tremendous pressure? That was the new question on everyone's lips.

Casey gave his now-historic answer to the press. "Don't worry about the kid. If this kid don't make out, I'll never call another shot in the rest of my days!"

Casey, the greatest manager in baseball, was putting his reputation on the line for an untried youngster! Could McGraw have felt any more certain when he first saw Ott? It was the kind of tribute that is paid to a rookie once in a lifetime.

It was also a tremendous responsibility for Mantle. He knew that when he stepped out on a big-league diamond for the first time, he would be alone. All the press praise wouldn't count. Even Casey's blessing wouldn't.

All that would count was Mantle himself—and the big bat he held in his hand.

As the train raced him toward New York and the great challenge, Mickey sat by himself, lost in thought. He spoke to no one and, after a time, the *clickity-clack, clickity-clack* of the wheels seemed to be saying to him, *The big leagues, the big leagues.*

"I mustn't fail," he told himself. "I *mustn't!*"

19

2.

ON the evening of October 20, 1931, two men sat hunched over a table in the small kitchen. Their expressions were gloomy, and they were obviously nervous.

Suddenly the bedroom door opened and a short man with shirt sleeves rolled up walked out. "Where is that second bag I brought with me? Oh, there it is." Then he picked up a small leather case and turned back toward the bedroom.

"One second, Doctor," said the younger man, jumping up. "How's my wife?"

"Fine," said the doctor.

"And my son?" The two men had heard the baby cry a few minutes earlier. "Is he okay?"

"What makes you think it's a son?" The doctor look half annoyed and half amused.

"It couldn't be anything else," answered the young husband.

"Well, you crazy young fathers get me," said the doctor, who was fond of saying that the young fathers were ten times more trouble to him than the young mothers. "But you're right. It's a boy."

"Is he all right?"

"He's all right enough for me to want to take him off your hands if you don't want him."

"Pop!" shouted the young man to the older man who was still seated. "Did you hear that? A boy! Just like we always wanted!"

"You two keep busy," said the doctor. "Talk baseball or something. I'll let you take a peek as soon as I get the mother ready."

The doctor's choice of a subject for them to discuss was not accidental. He knew them both well. Outside of caring for their families, he knew, they lived baseball winter and summer.

The younger man was Elvin C. Mantle. His friends affectionately called him Mutt. To support his family he worked as a lead and zinc miner, but he never let the back-breaking work or the poor wages depress him.

Mutt Mantle counted himself lucky to have the kind of good wife he'd always wanted. He was in good health. He was able, despite bad times, to keep a roof over his wife's head and food on the table. In addition, he spent his spare time playing baseball with every team in his part of Oklahoma that needed a player. He gleefully read every line of the sports papers and magazines. What more could a man want?

His father, Charles, was just like him. As a young man, Charles had been a pitcher for a semipro team. Never were father and son closer.

"Dad," said Mutt, "everything's beginning to move.

21

This is our chance. We got the boy—now all we have to do is make a ballplayer out of him."

"You know, son, some folks would consider us teched if they could hear us talk now."

"Why should they think that?" asked Mutt.

"The boy's just a few minutes old. It'll be quite a long time before he goes to school, let alone until he's old enough to catch a ball."

"Dad, it's like I've always said. You can't make a big-leaguer out of a young fellow two minutes before he's ready for a tryout. You've got to begin training him *before* he's old enough to catch or throw. He's got to *think* baseball right from the start. It's got to be part of his growing up."

"Well, son," said Charles, shaking his son's hand in congratulations, "maybe we'll fail at it. But we'll sure have ourselves one heck of a good time while we're trying!"

Mutt Mantle was beaming. At that moment, he was the happiest man in the entire universe.

When he went in to see his wife, she smiled and said, "Stop looking so worried. It's true what the doctor says—men take this even harder than women do. I'm tired right now, but I'm feeling fine." She looked toward the cradle which stood against her bed. "He looks just perfect."

"You saw him already?" Mutt asked.

"Did you think I'd wait for the doctor to send me a post card? I asked to see him the first thing. Then I counted his fingers and toes. I've never seen anything so beautiful."

"Me, neither," said Mutt. "What a ballplayer he'll make!"

His wife, in spite of her fatigue, burst out laughing.

"Mutt, Mutt, Mutt!" she said warmly. "I've sometimes thought that you're really married to baseball. But I guess I can't blame you. I'll bet our little boy will be able to do anything he wants to when he grows up."

Mutt's wife, Lovell Richardson Mantle, was an unusual woman. Back in those days before sports had yet caught on with any sizable number of women, she was a dyed-in-the-wool sports fan. To be sure, she didn't live it as did her husband, but she followed the teams closely. In high school she had been a champion runner. When she married Mutt, the neighbors in their little town of Spavinaw, Oklahoma (population 213), had commented that the marriage was made in heaven. Not only did they love each other, but they loved the same thing—sports.

"What are we going to call him, Mutt?" asked his wife. "I want to name him Charles after both our fathers."

"I don't have to tell you that nobody loves our two dads more than I do. But heck, you know what I want to call him."

"I thought maybe you changed your mind."

"Change my mind! A name is like an omen! Give him the name of a great ballplayer and he'll always know that he was born to be a player. Every time he signs his name, he'll be reminded."

23

"I still think he ought to be named Charles," said Lovell firmly.

"Tell you what," said Mutt. "I just got an idea. Let's give him Charles for a middle name."

"All right—if it'll make you happy. I guess our dads will understand."

And so the infant was named Mickey Charles Mantle. His first name was in honor of Mutt's baseball hero, Mickey Cochrane, who was at the time a catcher on the Philadelphia Athletics and one of baseball's all-time stars.

There is a little joke that the Mantle family likes to tell about this. It is that Cochrane's real name was Gordon Stanley Cochrane, but that Mutt hadn't known that. Actually, it probably wouldn't have mattered to him at all. Cochrane had become famous with the name Mickey, and that was the one he wanted his son to have.

When Mickey was several hours old, Mutt walked over to the cradle and held up a baseball. "Get a good look at it, sonny," he said, "you'll be seeing a lot more."

He wasn't joking. Other men who worked as hard as Mutt did in the mine, and who also had as little in a material way to show for it, would relax when they were off work. But not Mutt. From the minute that his son put in an appearance, he began to spend all his free time with the infant. He'd talk his heart out to him—as if the baby were able to understand.

"Mutt," his wife said to him one day. "There's something we have to talk about right now. We've got to make a decision."

"What's that, honey?"

"Well, we have to decide whether we'll use the cradle for the baby or for the baseballs. There's not enough room left for both."

Mutt blushed crimson. "I'll take some of the balls out," he said.

What he had done, when Mickey was just a few days old, was tuck a baseball into the corner of the cradle. He regarded it both as a good-luck omen and as a way of letting the baby know from the start that baseball was to be a big thing in his life. Besides, Mutt got a big kick out of seeing the ball and the baby so close together. Then he had put in another ball and still another, until half a dozen were tucked into various corners. And then Lovell had to call to his attention the fact that there could be too much of a good thing. So Mutt took some of the balls out.

The running chatter to the tyke about baseball never stopped. But when Mickey was three, Mutt decided not to neglect other aspects of the boy's education. Plainly it was time for his bright toddler to learn to count. But Mutt went about teaching him in a highly unusual way.

"This is *first* base," he would say, "this is *second,* and that's *third.* . . ." Or else he would throw up his hands and yell, "Strike *one*! Strike *two*! . . ." Slowly, little Mickey began to get the idea. And he also began to learn about baseball long before he realized that he was learning.

Naturally, a hard baseball is nothing for a tiny youngster to play with. He can be hurt too easily. So

Mickey's father substituted a rubber ball. "Let's throw it around," he'd say. Or, "Just try to tap it with this little stick. You don't have to hit it. Just get used to it."

A little later, as Mickey fondly recalls, he was the only boy in Spavinaw to have a real baseball uniform. It differed from a big-league uniform only in that it was pint-sized. But it was made from the same cloth, and was cut the same way. Where had Mutt obtained the midget uniform? The answer is that he had willingly sacrificed his own prized uniform and handed it to Lovell. She, in turn, had cut and sewed it into the real thing.

Mutt was delighted. "Mickey Cochrane himself," he said, "never looked more like a ballplayer than that."

And then, when Mickey was nearly six—and graceful and well co-ordinated for his age—Mutt said to his father, "Dad, do you think the time has come?"

"I guess so. He knows the fundamentals. Now let's teach him a real trick or two."

"Right!" said Mutt happily. Then he called for Mickey, who was standing with his mother. "Let's take a walk out to the field, son. Gramps and I want to show you something."

3.

"NOW we're about to play a little game, Mickey," Mutt said. "We couldn't play this game with you before because you were too little. But you're a big, six-year-old fella now."

It was good psychology. Every six-year-old wants to be thought of as grown up, and little Mickey was no exception. He beamed proudly.

"It's an easy game," said Mutt, handing him a dime-store bat. "When I throw to you, you just stand like this"—and he made Mickey face him right-handed. "Then when Gramps throws to you, you turn around like this"—and he moved the boy into a left-handed batting stance.

Then Mutt added: "And don't you worry none about getting hurt. This is just a soft little tennis ball. Could hardly hurt a flower, let alone a big, strong, six-year-old fella."

Today Mickey laughs when he recalls those first few batting sessions. He'd swing furiously at the ball but nothing much would happen. "It'll come," Mutt would say. "It's just a game." And Gramps would add: "Take your time, son. You got all the time in the world."

Comic as the sight would have been to any outsider

who watched, there was method in the seeming madness of Mutt and Gramps. They knew that a real ballplayer had to be trained from earliest childhood—they knew it was comparatively easy for a youngster to develop good baseball habits at an early age, and they didn't waste any time.

Many years later Casey Stengel was to tell the press, "This boy is the best switch-hitter that ever lived. The best, I tell you, and I've seen 'em all for forty years." The press itself was to nickname Mickey "the Sweet Switcher." But it all began on the day when Mickey was six and when Mutt and Gramps decided that the time had come.

By then the Mantles had moved from Spavinaw to Commerce, another mining town, which has less than 3,000 population today and had a lot less then. It was a more or less typical Oklahoma mining town. There were several blocks of store fronts, small buildings and houses, and the mines. The countryside was dotted with chat piles, or mounds of the waste materials from the mines. As the mining families knew, a waste heap is not the most beautiful sight in the world. But a town is mainly people, and, as in Spavinaw, the Mantles were lucky in their neighbors. The people of Commerce were warm, friendly, honest and hard-working. Poor or not, it was a good place for a youngster to grow up in.

Mutt's new job in the mine left him little free time. But, as before, his off-the-job hours were spent with the family.

Not a day went by without his teaching Mickey

something about baseball. Most times they would practice for an hour or so, but sometimes for much longer. The belief that Mickey would become a big-leaguer was no longer just a daydream for Mutt. It became such a certainty that he never let an opportunity go by without giving the youngster some coaching.

"How do you like his progress?" Mutt asked Gramps when Mickey was seven.

"Mutt, if I hadn't seen it from the start, I wouldn't have believed it. Sure, he's still a tiny little kid trying to hit a tennis ball, but I can hardly believe it's only a year since we put that bat in his hand. He's got a good smooth swing, and I like the way he runs. He's gonna be a ballplayer, and a good one."

The thing that amazed the two men was the co-ordination that young Mickey was developing. The other boys his age were awkward, and they moved in uneven, jerky motions when they fielded a ball or threw to a base. Mickey was smooth in action, and he was learning to wait patiently, developing a rhythm and an easy grace in his childlike batting form. He practiced day after day, and listened solemnly to his father's suggestions.

Mutt would talk to him as if he were really a grownup. Naturally, there was a lot that Mickey didn't understand. But he did understand that his father spent more time with him than the other fathers did with their kids. He understood that his father had tremendous confidence in him.

All this made Mickey begin to aim high. He began

to want, even at that early age, to bat and hit in a way that would make his dad even prouder of him.

"Mickey," said Mutt during this period, "I want you to know about a great player with the Giants and Cards called Frankie Frisch. Up to now, this Frisch fella has been the best switch-hitter. He was a left-handed hitter. He learned to hit right-handed because he figured that he would be a better hitter if he could bat both ways. He was right, because he learned to hit all kinds of pitching and became one of the great switch-hitters in baseball. Why, he even became a big-league manager—that's how smart Frisch was."

"One day you'll be a big-leaguer," Mutt would say. "Never forget that. Oh, there'll be days when you'll be discouraged. There'll be days when you'd rather play tag with the other kids or just lounge around and laze away the hours. But one day, when you see the rewards, you'll be glad you stuck to your ambition and worked hard. One other thing, Mick, when you feel too tired or lazy to practice, just remember that I want you to have a better chance than I had."

Mutt Mantle was a tender man. Some folks in Commerce saw only one side of him. They thought he was pushing the kid hard only because he was such a baseball "nut" himself. What they overlooked was that Mutt was more than a mere baseball fan. He was also one of the most devoted fathers in the town. He wanted his youngster to break out of the mining trap. He wanted him to get somewhere in life, to have a lot of the good things that Mutt never had.

And baseball, he was convinced, was the ladder to a better life for his son.

"Mickey," he would say, as the years passed, "do you know what every miner wants most when he's down under? He dreams about some fresh air and sunshine. It's not much—fresh air and sunshine. But when you're under the ground, it's the most important thing in the world. That's one of the reasons I like baseball so much. You play it out in the fresh air. You play it in summer when the sunshine pours over you. It's good and clean and it's the kind of life I want for you."

Sometimes he would say, "Mickey, you know that our house is built over a mine. So are plenty of other houses in this town. One day there could be a cave-in from a blast and the whole floor could fall out from under us. Oh, it won't happen. But it could. One day I want *you* living in a nice house on solid ground."

Mutt wanted the world for his son. He saw only baseball as the way out. So he poured his love and time and devotion into teaching his son everything he had learned about the game.

"Did you know, Mickey," he'd say, "that when you bat lefty you're two feet closer to first?" Do you know how many men get tagged out less than two feet from the base? What an advantage to bat lefty if you can! And there's nothing in the game to compare with a real switch-hitter. He's miles ahead before he starts!"

Mutt used his own meager spending money to buy tickets for local games. He'd sit there with an arm around his son and point out plays to the youngster that others in the stands were not seeing. Everything that he had learned in his lifelong study of the game he poured out to his boy.

Did all this hurt Mickey in his schoolwork? In his friendships with the other kids in the neighborhood?

The answer is that Mickey was one of the most popular boys in Commerce. The grownups liked him for his good manners. He was a modest youngster who always spoke to his elders respectfully and who always obeyed his parents. At the same time, the kids liked to pal with Mickey because he always had a happy grin and because he played ball as well as the bigger boys.

Mrs. Norma Pottorff was one of Mickey's first schoolteachers. She remembers him as having the "sweetest smile of any boy in my class."

Mrs. Pearl Miller, another Commerce teacher and a friend of the Mantle family, recalls that Mickey was very shy. But she also remembers that "Mickey was a boy who hated defeat. He could take it, but he didn't like it." Even in those early days, Mickey would pout and sulk after his team lost a game, but he would snap back quickly.

The person who remembers Mickey's determination best is his mother. One evening, a few years back, Milt Gross, the well-known sports scribe, was interviewing Mickey in his Commerce living room, when Mickey's mother joined the conversation.

"Mickey," she said, "I got to tell you something. Even when you were a little bitty thing you were never satisfied. . . . You got a single and you wanted a double. . . . You struck out fifteen batters and you wanted to strike out sixteen. Now it's the same."

"Ma," Mickey countered, "now I got to ask you something. That was the way Dad wanted it, wasn't it?"

"Yes, son. That's the way Pa wanted it."

"Then that's the way I want it, and I won't be satisfied until that's the way it is. He taught me one thing, and that is, never give up, never be satisfied. I'm just that way. I'm never giving up, and I'll always keep on trying to be better."

The big day for Mickey came when he was eleven years old. He was invited to play with his first uniformed team, the Douhat team in the Oklahoma peewee league. The Douhats had a regular schedule of games, and Mickey was the proudest boy in town when he suited up for the first time.

He was a catcher then—or he was trying to be. The idea, of course, was Mutt's. He was still patterning Mickey after Mickey Cochrane. But catching, as the whole town soon realized, wasn't Mickey's best position. He was faster than any kid his age. Squatting down behind the hitter throughout a game is obviously not putting such speed to its best use.

Mickey's mother laughs out loud to this day when she thinks of Mickey in that period. "He sure was small," she tells. "When he squatted down behind the bat wearing that protector that was too big for him, you couldn't see his feet. About all you could see of him, except for his arms, were those two little eyes sticking out of the protector like a scared turtle looking out of its shell."

And then Mrs. Mantle adds, "Soaking wet, he didn't weigh more than eighty-ninety pounds when he already was playing with boys almost as big as he is now."

One of his teammates in those days was Jack Myers, who still whiles away a winter evening with Mickey, now and then, playing dominoes. What kind of a peewee player was Mickey? "You know," Myers once told baseball writer Clyde Carley, "you were supposed to be between twelve and sixteen years old to play . . . Some were a little older but Mickey was only eleven. Still he was the best player we had."

The thing that Mickey himself remembers best about that time happened during one of the peewee games. Noticing that his father wasn't watching, he batted right-handed against a right-handed pitcher. Mutt had told him this was forbidden. He had to bat lefty against right-handed pitchers. Mickey thought he could get away with it just this once.

But Mutt, who had been sitting in the stands watching, walked up angrily. "Go home," he said, furiously, "and take off that uniform. Don't put it on again until you're ready to follow orders. You got to follow orders if you're gonna play as a team man."

After that, Mickey didn't try to put one over on Mutt again. Still, he kept developing ideas of his own and Mutt, even though he would sometimes argue fiercely with Mickey about them, was secretly glad. Mickey was beginning to think for himself—and Mutt had been waiting for that to happen.

He wanted the youngster to follow his advice, but he also wanted him to think independently. "A good ballplayer's got coaches, and scouts and a manager, and they'll all point out things for you," said Mutt, "but you start on the way to the big leagues when you think things out for yourself. Nobody can do your thinking for you, Mickey, nobody. You just remember that."

4.

ONE day while Mickey, who was then twelve, was playing for the Picher team in the Junior Cardinal League, he worked up his courage and had a talk with the team's manager.

"I don't think I'm in the right spot behind the plate," he said.

"Why not?"

"Well, I like to run. I like it when there's a lot of action. Behind the plate I just crouch all the time, and I think that I'm faster than the other guys, and I cover a lot more ground and field the position a lot better than the second baseman playing there now. I think we could tighten up the whole infield that way. We'd be a stronger team."

The manager studied him for a minute. He wasn't surprised by what Mickey was saying. He'd thought about it to himself in pretty much the same words. What amazed and amused him was the accuracy with which the youngster had analyzed the situation.

Just the night before he had said to a friend, "You know, the other kids take things as they come. They're just having fun, playing a game. But not this Mantle kid. Why, the kid's voice hasn't even changed yet, and yet he thinks about everything that he does in a baseball game from a long-range viewpoint—the way a real pro does."

Now he said to Mickey, "You are pretty fast. You're the fastest runner on the team, and I guess we could use your speed and strong arm elsewhere, and you're not a bad fielder."

Mickey beamed.

"What position do you want?" the manager asked.

"I'd like to try second base. If I'm no good at it, I can go back catching. I'll do my very best."

The manager laughed. "Okay," he said. "Especially since my regular second baseman got the mumps or chicken pox or something."

Later that day Mickey worked up his courage a second time and told Mutt about the change. He hadn't consulted with him about it and expected his father to hit the roof.

But Mutt wasn't annoyed. "It might be the right move," he said. "You're too fast a fella to be crouching behind the plate."

Mickey was happy. He and his father were even thinking alike now.

Then suddenly the daily life of the Mantles changed considerably.

Mutt had sold the house, and he added his life savings to what he had received, in order to lease some acres along a nearby river. He wanted to become a farmer in order to give his family more security than he had been able to, working in the mines in those hard years. He also wanted to make things pleasant for Grandpa Charles, who was ailing.

Then there was the fact that the Mantle family was growing. Besides Mickey, there were now three other sons—Theodore and twins named Roy and Ray.

It was a wise move and things started out great for the Mantles.

Mickey, who had always enjoyed hunting and fishing, loved his new surroundings. Mutt took to farming like a fish to water. Grandpa was comfortable. The Mantle kids loved the outdoors. And Mother Mantle was happy that everyone else was happy.

"It's nice out here, isn't it, Mickey?" Mutt would say.

"Great, Pa!"

"All the room in the world for batting a ball around, eh, son?"

"Even more space than in a big-league park!"

"Well," said Mutt, "we worked a long time for this and it feels good now that we've got it."

But the Mantles hadn't counted on Mother Nature Torrential rains, of a kind that no one had seen for years, soon turned into devastating floods that ruined the crops. The year was a complete financial loss and the land was a total wreck.

The Mantles were washed out. Worse, they were bankrupt. The family had no choice but to move back into a small hut, almost utterly lacking in conveniences on the edge of Commerce.

Fortunately, Mutt wasn't discouraged. He regarded

the episode as a temporary setback. He felt that it would be just a matter of time until some better breaks came along.

"What counts in life," Mutt told them, "is the same as in a baseball game. As long as we work together, stay together and keep our wits, that's the big thing. We'll start all over again, and I'm sure that we'll get going again. We've got a couple of innings left."

Mickey soon forgot the unhappy doings at home. He had made the first team at Commerce High School, and he was so excited that he could talk about nothing else. He was the regular pitcher on the team, and his fast ball was helping the team rack up a series of important wins. Soon the entire town was talking about that "Mantle kid."

More important was the fact that his batting had become the talk of the town. "The power in that kid's shoulders!" people would say. "Why, he hits 'em like a regular professional," one old-timer said.

When the baseball season ended, Mickey promptly went out for football. At first he was nonchalant about the game, but after several thrilling games with local schools he became as excited about the game as about baseball.

Mutt felt differently about it. "Football is all right," he told his son, "but not for someone whose future belongs to baseball. Football is a great game, but not for you. You use a different set of muscles. It can hurt your baseball playing."

"It keeps me in trim," Mickey would answer. "Keeps me from getting lazy. Besides, there's so much fun in it. I like to run with that ball, and to smack in and tackle a runner. It's a lot of good fun, Dad."

"It's too easy to get hurt in that game."

"Heck, Pop, that won't happen to me. I'll be real careful. Please, Pop, let me play. Honest, I won't ever let anything happen to hurt my baseball."

Soon, Mickey won from his teammates the same respect for his football playing that he had earned for his hitting and throwing on the baseball diamond.

John Lingo, who coached Mickey during his high-school days, called Mantle one of the finest players he had ever worked with. "I always rated him better at football than I did at baseball. I've seen about fifty All-Americans, and, in my opinion, none could touch Mickey. Why, he could kick and pass a football seventy yards! And run—why, once Mantle tucked that ball under his arm he was unstoppable. I've seen him race through an entire team for a score, and no one laid a hand on him, he was so fast."

Through the years, Grandpa Charles had encouraged Mickey only slightly less than Mutt. Now, as he lay ailing, he used his time to instill even more confidence in Mickey.

"Son, I can remember back to that day when your pa first showed you a baseball. You don't remember of course, and I guess it's a long time ago now. But to me it still seems like yesterday."

"I've heard about it so often," Mickey said, "I some times think I can almost remember it."

Grandpa laughed. "I guess your pa and me must've looked silly to a lot of folks. Maybe we still do. I don' know, and I guess it doesn't matter. The important thing is that we were *right*. You have a great baseball career ahead of you."

"I hope so."

"It's not just hope that'll get you there. It's the stuff —whatever it is that makes a man a natural big-leaguer —and you've got it. I always wished that I had it, all the time when I played ball. But I didn't and I faced the fact. Mutt played his heart out—but he didn't have it. But you do! And you can take the word of this old codger for that!"

"You're not so old, Gramps."

Grandpa Charles laughed. "What do young fellows know about age? Only old fellows know how it feels to have the years hang heavy."

"Ah," said Mickey, "you talk like that only because you've been feeling a little sick lately. You'll be better in no time."

"Probably you're right," said his grandfather, who knew better. "One thing, though, I want you to always remember is that you're big-league stuff through and through. No matter how discouraged you become, don't ever forget what I'm telling you. Your true road is right up to the top. Yes, right up to that high place where a man can live a clean and honest life away from the mines. Never lose sight of that!"

Shortly after, Grandpa Charles died, and Mickey and Mutt felt as if the ceiling had come down on them. The three of them had been like three pals of the same age. When they were talking baseball, there was no difference in years between them.

41

First the floods and bankruptcy, then Grandpa's death. What else could possibly happen to the Mantles?

The third misfortune was not long in coming. It happened during a regular high-school football practice session. And at first it seemed as if nothing at all had happened. Another high-school football player accidentally kicked Mickey in the leg. That was all. Surely nothing to make a fuss about.

"It's just a little sprain," Mickey told Mutt as he limped home.

"Does it hurt a lot?" his father asked him.

"Hardly at all. My ankle's a little raw. Nothing even worth noticing. I'll soak it and go to sleep. It'll be like new in the morning."

But it wasn't. And one day the result of that kick in the leg was to make national headlines.

5.

"HOW'S the ankle, Mickey?" Mutt asked the next morning.

Then, before Mickey could answer, he lifted the cover to take a look. "Holy cow! How could you sleep with an ankle like that?"

"I couldn't. I tossed around all night. It hurts like the devil."

Mutt was staring at his son's leg and he turned pale. Mickey's ankle was nearly twice its ordinary size and nearly black.

"Can you hop to the car if you hold onto my shoulder? We can't fool with this. We've got to get you to the doctor at once. I'd have taken you last night if I had any idea that it was as bad as this."

The doctor in town examined Mickey and then sat facing them. "I don't know what to tell you," he said.

"Why not, Doc?" asked Mutt.

"Because I don't know what it is."

There was no bluff in the doctor's manner. He was a good, small-town doctor and he always said exactly what was on his mind. "I just don't have the X-ray equipment here to make a thorough examination."

"Well, which doctor in town has it?"

"Mutt, no one here has the equipment. Your best bet is to go to the hospital or the Eagle Lead Company in Picher. The doctors there will be able to make a correct diagnosis. Don't waste time. Get going now."

"Let's go, Mickey," said Mutt, helping his son up.

In the car, Mickey said, "I still don't see how a little kick could swell the leg up like that. It didn't even hurt at first. I mean it didn't hurt any more than if you stumble into a piece of furniture or something."

"We'll soon find out, son. Probably they'll give you a few shots and you'll be all right. But it sure goes to prove what I said about football. I told you not to play. I begged you to stick with baseball. We wouldn't have this now if you'd listen to me."

"Heck, Pop, it could have happened in any sport. Or even while taking a walk in the street. It was just a tough break, Pop. You know how those things happen."

The hospital of the lead company was well equipped. The doctors examined Mickey and then busied around with him for hours. Finally, Mutt was asked to step into the office of one of the doctors for a private chat.

"This is no minor injury that your boy has, Mr. Mantle," the doctor said.

"What is it?"

The physician peered at Mutt, as if to see whether he was a man who could take bad news without sugarcoating. "I'll give it to you straight," he finally said. "Your son has osteomyelitis."

"What on earth is that?"

"It's a pretty serious bone disease, Mr. Mantle, and

it's a mighty serious condition that your boy is in at this moment."

As the doctor explained, the kick on Mickey's left shin had caused the blood to clot right next to the bone. The clot, in turn, had become swollen and infected with bacteria.

"How will this affect his future health, Doctor? Will he be okay? Will he be able to work, or play ball? Tell me, please, Doctor. It's important."

"We can't say, Mr. Mantle. These things take different turns with different people. But this demands expert treatment. We can only diagnose him here and treat him for the moment. But you'd better make arrangements for longer treatment as soon as you can."

"Thank you," Mutt said, as he went to fetch his son.

Back home, Mutt seemed to be like a man lost in a dream. Then he disappeared from the house for many hours. When he came back, he said to Mickey:

"All right, fella, I have it now."

"You have what, Dad?"

"I have enough money to take you to the best hospital in Oklahoma City for treatment. I've been busy raising all I could."

Mickey spent the next few weeks in a hospital bed, and it was torture for him. He received injections around the clock. And when he wasn't receiving injections, he was being baked by various diathermy machines.

"I don't really mind," he told his parents when they visited. "Knowing that I'll be as good as new when I get out of here cheers me up a lot."

And then, when it was time to leave, Young Mickey got it right between the eyes. The doctor said it gently. "You're lucky, son, but I'm afraid you'll never play ball again. You'll have to take these home with you." His parting souvenir was a pair of crutches!

But not until he was home again did the full meaning of his illness hit him. He would not be able to play ball again! He felt as if someone had told him that he wouldn't be able to breathe again.

"Heck," Mutt said, in order to console him, "there's things in this world besides ball playing."

"Sure, there are. But without being able to hit one, and stretch a single into a double, and field one that you were sure you'd miss— Oh, you know what I mean, Dad."

"Yes, I do, son. Yes, I do. Just you get well. That's all for now." And then Mutt would try his best to look cheerful in order to keep up his son's morale.

But his osteomyelitis was, as Mickey soon found out, a peculiar condition. It came and went—or seemed to go. There would be days when he would feel fine. The leg wouldn't bother him at all. He'd walk on it, and there would be no pain. Then he'd run and still no pain. And yet, at other times, indescribable pain would jolt through his leg even though he barely moved it.

Mickey felt as if his life were over. For years he had been preparing for a big-league career—a career of excitement, of slashing base hits, crowds, fame and glory. Now, all he could do was lie in bed.

But Mickey's love for sports was too strong to allow

him to give up. On days when the leg seemed "sound," he'd get out of the house and soon pitch himself into a ball game as if nothing were wrong with him at all. More amazing was the fact that he started to play football again. Why? Because he loved the game and because he didn't like the idea of thinking that an injury had chased him away from it.

Time went by in this way. Playing ball, and never knowing when his leg would give out—a ballplayer who often had to limp on crutches when he wasn't playing! How many young athletes would have permitted themselves to engage in any physical activity under such conditions?

"Well," he told his father one day as they sat around, "at least I can still get a little fun out of playing ball."

"So long as you remember to favor that leg, Mickey. It's nothing to fiddle around with. Just forget about playing ball. It's too dangerous. You've got to take it easy."

"I stop when I feel a little tired. I just can't keep staying in the house, Dad. I'll go nuts. I got to try it out. Maybe strengthen it a little. Just a little playing every other day. Maybe that's all it needs—a little exercise."

And then one day, to give Mickey's sagging spirits a lift, Mutt took him on a long drive to see the St. Louis Cards play in the World Series. It was a day that the youngster would never forget. He drank in every detail of the exciting moments of the Series and never took his eyes off the great stars, Stan Musial and Big

47

Mort Cooper. He hungrily watched Marty Marion make those great plays at shortstop for the Cards; and when Enos Slaughter dashed madly around the bases, the excited youngster could hardly contain his excitement. He studied every move that was made on the field. He thrilled to every hit, and his heart fell with every strike-out or error.

"Having a good time, son?"

"Gee, yes, Pop! Boy, am I glad that you brought me. This is the best game I've ever seen! Gosh, it's the greatest thing that ever happened to me."

"Good, good," said Mutt quietly. He was glad that his son could still enjoy watching others play without feeling too much pity for himself, without thinking too much about his great misfortune.

And then, when the game was over, Mickey turned toward his father. His face was flushed, but he wasn't smiling.

"Dad," he said in deadly earnest, "you give those crutches away today. I won't need them any more. My sideline days are over. I intend to play all-out baseball from now on! I don't care what happens, I just got to get out on the field again. I got to get my leg better, and I'm not ever going to use those crutches again."

6.

"IT'S worth a try," the Commerce High School football captain told the huddled players. "We're behind by three points and time is running out. Back to your positions!"

The center snapped the ball to the quarterback, who spun to the left with the ball. When the other team broke through and went after him, he lateraled to halfback Mickey Mantle, who smacked into the line and then stopped short. Two of the opposing players were waiting for him, ready to smack him down for a loss on the play.

Making a split-second decision, Mantle ran straight up to the first player, faked him out of position and dashed toward the sideline. Suddenly he cut sharply upfield toward the goal line, and he was out in the clear all by himself. It was a beautiful play to watch, and the crowd roared as Mantle raced up the field with the pack of players at his back. Thirty, forty yards he sped, and then in a final burst of speed he was over for the touchdown.

"What a run, Mickey!" his teammates yelled, as they hugged him. "Seventy-five yards! We win the championship! Yeah, Mickey!"

The Commerce High football team won that game, and they knew that Mickey had given them the victory. The pats of congratulations that he got when the game was over nearly gave him a sore back.

Running out of the T formation, Mantle was the sensation of the Commerce High football team in his senior year. His great speed and shiftiness made it difficult for the opposing teams to bring him down. He was the triple-threat sensation of the year, and he led the team in scoring, racing for ten touchdowns. Game after game was won by a long, twisting Mantle run or a tremendous Mantle pass for a touchdown, and before the season was over the college football scouts were offering the fleet football star scholarships to every Midwestern college.

But the thing that pleased Mickey Mantle most was his father's reaction after a thrilling Mantle touchdown run. He knew that after the game was over Mutt would tell him that playing football was a darn-fool thing for him to do. But Mickey would prefer to remember the broad grin that covered Mutt's face as he saw his son race down the field.

Back home, Mutt said, "Ready for the treatment?"

"I guess so."

"Then lay down here and get that leg uncovered."

The bone disease was still with Mickey. It hadn't got better. He still had to go to see the doctor more often than other kids went to see the Western in the local movie house, and he had to submit to other daily fussing with the leg at home. In that year, also, it was necessary for him to re-enter the hospital for several stays.

His leg hadn't got better. He had merely learned to live with it better. He had fought it as if it were a personal enemy. He had continued to play ball as if nothing were wrong with his leg—praying all the time that it wouldn't conk out in the middle of a game.

Not only did he choose to play football again, but he also added basketball to his list of conquered sports. Bad leg or not, he had not lost one whit of his incredible speed.

But his first love was baseball. He knew by then that playing baseball was the most important thing in his life.

Little did Mickey know, however, as he drove himself in spite of a trick leg, that the sun of good fortune was about to shine on him. Just as bad breaks had piled up one on top of the other, now the good breaks were coming. And they also came in bunches. The first break came in the shape of Barney Barnett.

Barney Barnett was a boss in the mines and also one of the organizers of the Ban Johnson League, a famous amateur baseball tournament that operated in several states. He knew professional baseball men by the dozen. They respected what Barney was doing, and they knew that he had real baseball savvy. Many a player who went on to bigger things started out in the B-J league.

One day, Barney (who had known Mutt Mantle for many years) got a look at Mutt's boy in action. Mickey was then playing second base for the Miami, Oklahoma, team in the Ban Johnson league. Barney was managing the Baxter Springs Whiz Kids in the same league. As it turned out, Barney saw Mickey humiliated.

There were three men on as Mickey stepped up to bat. A single would have driven in at least one run and probably two. A homer would have cleared the bases.

But, on a hunch, Barney had signaled his infielders to move to the edge of the infield. Mickey took a terrific clout at the ball and drove it straight at the shortstop, who caught the ball, stepped on second base for the second out and then whipped the ball to home plate for the third out. It was a tremendous play, and the crowd roared with approval as three Miami players had gone out in a lightning bang-bang play.

Mickey, with the bases loaded, had hit into a triple play!

After the game, Mutt prepared himself for a few jeers when he saw his old friend, Barney Barnett, walking toward him.

"It could've happened to anyone," Mutt said, trying to take the sting out of what Barney would say. "But it happened to my boy, so I guess I'll have to listen to you crack about it. I guess we got it coming."

"Mutt," said Barney, "that boy of yours is a real hitter. I like the way he stands up there at the plate and takes his cut at the ball! And he's got real power."

"Sure has. He cleaned the bases all right. Not exactly a good day for him, but I guess it could happen to anyone."

"I'm serious, Mutt. That stance, that natural swing, that follow-through! Why, the kid's got the making of a real pro. Needs a lot of coaching, but he's got real class."

Mutt perked up his head. "You're not kidding about this, are you Barney?"

"Kidding? Since when do I kid when I come across a youngster with real promise? Don't you know that your kid's out of the ordinary?"

"Sure I know it," Mutt said, "but, after all, he did hit into a triple play and I was sure you were coming over to razz me."

"What does one play matter? That form! Golly, it's *thrilling* to see it in a kid player! Just think—with some real coaching and concentration on one position, that boy of yours could go a long way in baseball."

"Glad you feel that way, Barney. I've felt like that since the day that little Mickey used to lay peacefully in his crib. Of course my boy's gonna play in the big leagues one day."

"Mutt, I want you to turn him over to me."

"Exactly what are you proposing, Barney?" Mutt said, and his expression showed that he was all business now.

"I want him to join my team in Baxter Springs. Heck, the Miami team he's playing for is folding up, anyway, after this season."

"You'll keep a sharp eye on him, and take good care of him?"

"My word of honor, Mutt. In fact, nothing on this earth could keep me from doing that. I'm going to give that boy of yours all my attention. I just can't believe my eyes. Why that boy is almost ready for a semipro team right now. A little hard work, plenty of rest and good food, and we've got ourselves a ballplayer."

"I'll have to talk to Mickey about it."

"You do that, Mutt," Barney said. "I think this is the start of big things for him."

Later that evening Mutt told Mickey about Barney's offer. "The decision is yours to make," he added.

Mickey looked thoughtful but didn't say anything. "Pop, you know how it is with us. You're the boss. What do you say about this? Sounds okay to me."

"I don't have to tell you," Mutt said, "that Barney's a fine man. He's also a real baseball man. Knows the game through and through. Also he's got contacts with a lot of the big-league players and scouts. And, Mickey, he likes you an awful lot."

"What are we waiting for, Dad?" Mickey said. "Let's tell him Yes before he changes his mind."

Mickey knew from the start that this was a real break.

As a member of the Whiz Kids, Mickey was switched to shortstop, and he soon got the hang of the new position. Barney taught him all he knew about the position, and Mickey took to the older man's teachings. He got a big bang out of riding around in a bus to all the little towns in which they played.

"This is just like the big leagues, I'll bet," one of the other players said one night on the bus.

"I don't see how any team can get fancier treatment than this," Mickey answered.

It was the life! Great times, great games, great fun! Not a boy in the country wouldn't have eaten it up.

And it was all possible because one man named Barney Barnett had wanted the kids to have it.

But, in addition to pouring advice into Mickey's ears, Barney kept his word and let everyone who would listen know about Mickey's great playing. He not only talked to scouts when they passed through the territory, but then went home and wrote letters to the home offices of the baseball clubs.

Still, nothing happened. But Barney assured Mickey that something would, soon enough. "It's just a matter of time," he would say.

Baseball umpire Kenny Jacobson spotted Mickey's playing during a series in Joplin. After the games he cornered the youngster and said, "Tell me, son, have you ever tried out for a team in a higher league? I think you'd be a good bet for one of the teams in Class D ball. What do you think about it, Mickey?"

"Mr. Jacobson," said Mickey, "I can say honestly that I've never done anything else in my whole life. It's been baseball with me all the day."

"I've been watching you, and, in my opinion, you're no ordinary sand-lot player. If you don't mind, I'd like to make a suggestion."

"Why should I mind, Mr. Jacobson? I'd sure appreciate it."

"Then go over to Joplin and talk to Johnny Sturm. He's the manager of the New York Yankees' farm club and a real right guy. Tell him you'd like to try out for a spot on his club. It can't hurt, and maybe it can lead to something."

"I'll talk to my father about it, Mr. Jacobson, and I'm sure he'll say all right."

Mutt thought it was a very good idea. So Mickey, who idolized the Yankees, hitchhiked to Joplin, some thirty miles away.

"Sure, I'll look you over," Sturm said when Mickey got there. "Get into this Joplin outfit. But I'm afraid you'll have to use your own shoes."

"Thank you very much," Mickey said, running to get into the suit.

Sturm watched him work out on the field for a few days and then asked Mickey how old he was and how his education was coming.

"I'll be seventeen soon, and I'll graduate in a few weeks."

"Pretty smart lad, to be getting out at seventeen."

"Nah," Mickey said, with a shy grin, "it's just that I started school a year earlier than the other kids— when I was five instead of six. Probably my dad figured that would give me an extra year to play baseball in."

"Smart dad you've got," Sturm said smiling.

"Do you think I have a chance to make your team, Mr. Sturm?" Mickey asked.

Sturm was encouraging but noncommittal. "You're not bad at all," he said. "Not bad at all. But I'll have to see more of you. Tell you, son, you go on home, and I'll think about it."

So even though nothing had happened, Mickey went home with his head in the clouds. A big-league man had thought that he wasn't bad at all! How much more encouragement could a young ballplayer want?

Yankee scout Tom Greenwade, a lean, bony-faced man with long years in the game, had heard about Mantle. But he wanted to see the boy in action. The Yanks were interested in Mickey—at least to the extent of taking another look—and Greenwade was the man who was to do the looking.

He went to Alba, Missouri, to see Mickey and Baxter Springs play the Alba Aces. But Tom admits that he wasn't too impressed with Mickey. There were several other players who interested him more. But he made a mental note to watch Mickey play again.

The game that Greenwade chose to watch him in next was one in which the Baxter Whiz Kids played Coffeeville. But this one nearly didn't come off. That is, Mickey nearly missed being in it.

The trouble was that Mickey was to graduate at the same hour that the game was to start. Obviously, he couldn't be on the school stage getting his diploma and at the same time be on the field playing for the Whiz Kids—and Greenwade.

But a place like Commerce abounds in friends, friends of the kind who take it upon themselves to do things for a fellow in a jam. One such friend was Johnny Lingo, the school coach. He ran breathless into the office of the high-school principal.

"Look," he said, "there's a big-league scout from the New York Yankees in town to watch Mickey Mantle play. The whole town knows about it. But Mickey has to be in the auditorium to get his diploma. Can't we do something about it?"

"Such as what?"

"Heck, it's only a formality, stepping up to the stage. Mickey's diploma is filled out already. This is a chance of a lifetime for him. Couldn't we give him his diploma now?"

"I don't see why not. It is already filled out. Why, I've got it right here."

Muttering "Thanks," Lingo rushed over to the Mantle house. He handed the diploma to Mutt and said, "Tell Mickey to get ready for the game. We'll all be rooting for him."

Mickey played in that game. He got four hits, and made three errors.

"I'll be around to watch you again," said Greenwade.

True to his word, he showed up a week later, and watched Mickey in another game. The Whiz Kids were hitting against Coffeeville's best left-handed pitcher. When it came his turn at bat, Mantle stepped up to the plate and, batting right-handed, lashed out a screaming double. In the fourth inning Mickey turned around, this time against a right-handed pitcher, and batted left-handed. He waited for a good pitch and laced out another two-base hit.

Tom Greenwade, sitting in the stands with Mickey's father, turned to Mutt. "He hit from both sides of the plate all the time. Funny I didn't notice it before."

"Been doing it since he was six years old," Mutt said. "I made him do it. Figured it would make him twice the hitter, and he hits them long ones, too."

Then the heavens broke and rain finished baseball

for that day. In order to get away from the downpour, Mickey and Mutt ran toward their car, and Greenwade jumped into the car with them.

"How would you like to sign a Yankee contract for your boy?" Greenwade asked Mutt.

"I might be interested."

"Well, I got Independence in mind for him. That's Class D. I'd like him to finish out the rest of this 1949 season over there."

"What's his future after that?"

"Joplin, Class C, if he makes out with Independence."

"How much are you offering?"

"One hundred and forty a month."

Mutt shook his head. "That won't do. He'll be working in the mines this summer, and he'll be getting fifteen dollars a Sunday for playing ball. That comes to more than you're offering."

"Well, let's see," said Greenwade, taking out a pencil. "I can add a bonus of eleven hundred dollars, for signing, to that hundred and forty per month. But that's as far as I can go. Take it or leave it!"

"What say, Mickey?" Mutt asked.

"It's up to you, Dad."

"Then let's go ahead, son."

Sitting there in the pouring rain, Mickey and his dad signed the contract with the famous New York Yankees. When the signing was over, Mutt slowly reached over, put his arm around Mickey's shoulder and said, "Boy, now you're on your way. You're out of the mines for good. Thank God for that!"

7.

MICKEY wiped the perspiration out of his eyes with the back of his hand, hunched his back and then lifted his arms over his head. Finally, he picked up the bat and stepped up to the plate.

"Look, fellas, if it ain't the wind beater again!" razzed a player on the opposing team.

"C'mon, Mick, belt it out of the park!" yelled one of Mickey's Independence teammates. "You're the guy to do it!"

Mickey stared at the pitcher. He hoped the hurler didn't know how wound up he was inside. The bat didn't feel right on his shoulder. His arms seemed suddenly to be made of concrete, and he felt as if he were waving two stiff slabs when he made his practice swings. The perspiration was clouding his eyes again.

It was a tense moment for everyone watching, and unbearable for Mickey. It was the last inning with two out and a man on second. A clean hit would bring him home from second and tie the game. A homer would end it.

Why did this have to be my turn up? Mickey thought. He knew he had been playing badly. In his first ten games for Independence, he had gone hitless.

" 'Way over the fence this time, Mick!" boomed his teammate to him. "We're counting on you!"

"I'll do it," Mickey suddenly told himself. "I'll do it. The next one that comes over—I'll smash the guts out of it!"

The next one was a ball, high and outside.

"Just bring it in low and a little on the inside," Mickey said to himself, almost aloud. "Just let it come across over here and . . ."

Standing there waiting for the pitcher to finish his windup was painful.

The pitch came in fast and on the inside. Mickey swung. It was a tremendous effort. He put so much power into it that he nearly pitched face forward to the ground.

"Strike three!"

He was out. He had struck out again. The team had counted on him and he had gone down like a duffer who had never played ball before.

"Bye-bye, wind beater!" yelled the player who had razzed him as the winning team embraced in victory. Mickey felt his face flush burning hot, and he started angrily toward the player.

"Hold it, kid!" said a man who walked out of the dugout. "A talk between you and me is a little over-due. Let's get around to it right now." Then the man motioned for Mickey to walk with him to the out-field.

The man was Harry Craft, manager of the Independence team. He knew baseball inside out. He had played it, managed it, and lived it all his life. His active years on the field had been with the Cincinnati Reds in the late thirties and early forties. His best batting average had been .257, but the figure alone didn't in the slightest tell the story of the man's mastery of the game. It was his know-how that had convinced the Yanks to send Craft to Independence. They felt sure that if any promising kid with real stuff came along, Harry would be able to get the best out of the youngster, help him and bring him along slowly.

"I tried my best," Mickey said when they reached the outfield. "I guess I'll never make the grade here. Can't do anything right, I guess. But I can take bad news all right. You won't need to give me a speech with my walking papers, Mr. Craft. I'll always remember all the time you took trying to teach me. I don't know. I guess I'm not good enough. I belong back in Commerce."

"Don't talk crazy, kid," Craft said. "Sit down on the grass here. I'm not sending you home or anywhere. I just want to shoot the breeze a little with you, like I said."

"But I didn't get a hit in ten games! Ten whole games and not even one miserable single! They sent me here because they thought I could hit. I was sure I could hit since I was in short pants. But I see now I was hitting only because I was playing against little kid teams. This is a real pro team. Ten days I've been here and I would've given my right arm to get on base once. Just once! I guess the fellas on the other team got me tagged right when they called me a wind beater."

"I said knock it off, kid," said Craft sternly. "Sit down on the grass like I told you. I brought you out here to talk to you in private as if you were my own kid. But for a quiet guy you're sure talkative all of a sudden."

Mickey stopped talking and sat down.

"First, I'll tell you the good news. Maybe it'll help you to ease up on yourself a little. You're wound up tighter than a top." Craft sat down beside Mickey and talked to him in a softer voice. "I've watched you swing at the air in ten games now. On the record, I'd tell you to take up knitting. But one day you'll be a big-leaguer. I'm sure of that. One day you'll laugh about how you couldn't get a hit in Independence."

"You're kidding me, Mr. Craft."

"When I'm kidding you, I'll tell you," Craft said, chuckling. "Besides, I don't go around telling duffers they got big-league stuff in them. It's even dangerous to tell it to a young fella who's really got it. It's such a long way up there to the Yankee Stadium and a lot of guys break up inside when it finally dawns on them they'll never make it. No, I wouldn't kid anybody about a thing like that."

Mickey's face showed his bewilderment, but he knew better than to talk at that moment.

"Mickey, you're trying too hard," Craft said. "That's the long and short of it. You're not only not hitting, you're doing a dozen things wrong. Got the stomach, boy, to listen to me take you apart piece by piece?"

Mickey nodded.

"Your big trouble is that you're trying too hard.

You've got to get up there and face every pitch nice and loose. Try to chew gum or think of a funny story. Laugh it up a little. You got a free and easy swing that's got to produce a lot of runs for us, but nice and easy. Another thing you've got to learn—the other team is going to jeer you plenty of times, and you got to be able to answer back, not with wisecracks, but with base hits. That's what you do. And stop trying to hit homers every time your chance to bat rolls around. Just get a piece of the ball. Meet the ball squarely; that's the important thing. And when you relax, those arms and shoulders of yours will do the rest with the big pitches.

"Keep your arms at your side. You're the fastest runner I ever saw, but still, you look like a drowning swimmer. And even when you hit a long one, don't ever—I mean *ever*—take your eyes off that ball."

"There's an awful lot I still got to learn," Mickey said, his eyes full of thanks for the help Craft was trying to give him.

"It's always the little things, Mickey. Not only in baseball, but in everything folks do. Remember the old saying about if you watch the pennies the dollars will take care of themselves. Stretch a single by starting to run the second you slam the ball, cut first fast, and soon you'll find yourself with two-baggers. Heck, relax a little, and you'll find hitting homers here is not a heck of a lot harder than with the Whiz Kids. Sure, the competition is tougher, but each year—for at least a few years—you'll be getting taller and stronger."

Then Craft's whole face lit up in a laugh. "How do

you like that? The kid's all of seventeen years old and he was sure I was washing him out of baseball!" Turning to Mickey, he added, "One day I'll remind you about that. We'll bust our sides laughing about it together!"

Craft knew what he was talking about. Despite his slow start, Mickey began banging the ball as if he were with the Whiz Kids again. As the season roared to a climax, Mickey found himself the talk of the K-O-M (Kansas-Oklahoma-Missouri) League in which Independence played. His .322 average for the season didn't tell the story, for he had arrived at Independence in the middle of the season, and the slump with which he had started kept his final averages down. Nevertheless, his .322 average was only a few points away from the league lead, and fully half of his drives had been for extra bases.

Back home for the winter, Mickey went to work in the mines under the supervision of his dad. Mutt was the ground boss at the Blue Goose Number 1 mine, and Mickey put in a full day's work alongside his dad, and they talked baseball all the time.

And then, in the middle of the winter, a real thrill came in the mail. The home office of the Yankees wrote to tell Mickey that they were setting up a special pre-season training school at Phoenix, Arizona, for some promising young players and they wanted him to attend when February rolled around.

"I couldn't've done so bad," he told Mutt. "They wouldn't invite me if I made out as bad as I thought. Isn't that right?"

65

"Right as rain," said Mutt. "What on earth's so bad about nearly leading the league in batting your first year with Independence? Fella, you didn't even put the uniform on until half the season was over. You didn't even get a chance to work out with them or nothing. You just got dumped in out of nowhere. And you still did great!"

"Pop, it would sure be swell if everybody was as positive about how good a ballplayer I am as you are. I wish I was, myself!"

"You'll go great up at Phoenix. There ain't a real baseball man around who got to do more than just take a look at you handling the bat. Boy, I've been telling you since the day you drank milk right out of the bottle you'll be way up there one day. Maybe now you're starting to believe it a little, that your old man knows what he's talking about."

"It's still a plenty-long way away from the Yankee Stadium, Dad."

"Oh, just a few seasons," said Mutt airily. "Even sooner if the Yankee home office got as much baseball sense as I think they got."

Mickey and the other rookies stayed in Phoenix for only two weeks. They had barely arrived when Baseball Commissioner "Happy" Chandler handed down a ruling which held that the Yankee school was no more than a gimmick for starting spring training early. So the Yanks had to send the rookies back home.

But not before they got their first good look at Mickey. Stengel's coaches at the school were Frank Crosetti, Bill Dickey and Jim Turner. All of them were amazed by Mantle's hustle and walloping ability. They all raved to Casey about him.

"Keep a special eye on him, Casey," they said. "The kid's 'way out of the ordinary. And he's just a baby. He got a whole lifetime in baseball ahead of him."

Mickey's speed soon caught Casey's attention. Casey had always tried to get across to players the value of a quick start and hustle between the bases.

"I been seein' you runnin' the other players ragged," Casey told Mickey one day.

Casey was referring to the short sprint races that the rookies ran a dozen times a day. His orders to the coaches were to keep the rookies off their backsides. "Teach 'em where they got their feet," Casey had said, "and maybe they'll figure out themselves where their head is hanging."

"I like to run," Mickey answered. "It gets the lead out of my feet. Wakes me up a lot. And Mr. Craft keeps reminding me a lot of games are won with the feet, and not only with hits."

"You keep your ears plugged in to Harry Craft. He knows this game good as anyone."

"He sure knows his stuff," Mickey agreed.

And then Casey got off the remark to Mickey that became famous. "Just keep chasin' them rabbits, sonny boy, and you'll be all right."

The good news for Mickey came just as the training school broke up. He was told that his salary had been raised to $250 per month and that he would play Class C ball for Joplin in the season coming up. He was excited to learn that Harry Craft was also being promoted to Joplin as manager and, as Yankee insiders knew, Mantle's tutor.

Mickey raced back to Commerce bursting with confidence. To help the family income along, he took a job in the mines. But he couldn't wait for the season to start. His impatience was so great that, long before each day was over, he would tear another page off the calendar that hung on the Mantles' kitchen wall.

Then, when the great day arrived, he showed up in Joplin with a zest he hadn't had at the start of the Independence season. Soon, the Class C Western Association buzzed with talk about eighteen-year-old Mickey Mantle who was burning his way through the league. Halfway through the season the Commerce Comet was hitting the ball at an amazing .414 average. Nobody could stop the nimble-footed Mantle as he raked the pitchers from either side of the plate.

"Listen to this, fellas," Tom Greenwade, the Yankee scout, told home-office staffers in New York. "You'll get a real bang out of it. I was talking to one of the managers of a team in the Western Association. His team played against Joplin the night before and he had Mickey Mantle on his mind. 'Tom,' he told me, 'we had pretty good luck with this Mantle kid last night. He got four hits, but they were all singles.' Can you beat that? Mantle gets on base against his team four times in one game and the guy's happy. He's happy Mantle didn't pop four homers!"

At season's end, Mickey's average with Joplin was a fabulous .383. He also had driven in 136 runs and hit twenty-six homers—fourteen left-handed and twelve right-handed! He not only won the league's batting championship but walked away with the Most Valuable Player award!

"We'll be expecting you to show up for spring training next year," the Yankee office told Mickey when the season was over.

He was to go to Phoenix again! And this time not as a student in a school for rookies, but as a rookie working out with the Yankee team itself! He would get a chance to meet Joe DiMaggio and all his other Yankee heroes, and have a chance to show them what he could do!

Once again Mickey could not wait for the winter to pass.

8.

WHEN the Yankee club counted all the rookies at Phoenix in 1951, they found that one was missing. Mickey Mantle was nowhere in sight.

"Where the devil is that kid?" asked Yankee general manager George Weiss. "That doesn't sound like that boy, not being here on time."

"Probably lost somewhere between here and Oklahoma," another answered. "You know how lost those farm boys are when they get off the farm."

"Let's not gab about it," said Johnny Neun, a Yankee scout. "Let's find out."

So Neun got on the phone and called Mickey in Commerce. "What in blazes are you doing down there?" he thundered. "You're supposed to be up here."

Mickey was silent for a moment. And then he stammered, "I just don't—I don't have enough money to get there."

"Then why in heck didn't you call or write and say so! Do you expect us to hold up spring training until next winter? I'll wire you the money as soon as I hang up. Get your bags packed now and hop on the train the minute the Western Union boy walks in with the money."

"My suitcase—it's been packed for a month."

When Mickey arrived at the Phoenix camp, he felt as if he were stepping into wonderland. It was a dream come true.

"Hey, look!" he shouted to rookie pitcher Tom Morgan a few hours after he came, "there's Joe DiMaggio!"

"In person!" said Morgan. "I'll introduce you. Joe and I are old friends."

Mickey looked at the young hurler with new respect. "You know Joe a long time?"

"I just met him two days ago," was the laughing answer. "And don't let me kid you. I was just as thrilled as you."

"I feel like pinching myself to see if I'm really here," Mickey said. "Last year when I came up to the rookie school the regular team wasn't here yet. Now I'll be throwing a ball around and hitting with the real team. It just doesn't feel real. I'm afraid one of these days I'll pinch myself, wake up and find that I've been dreaming about all this."

"I'll tell you this," said Morgan, who was two or three years older than Mickey. "I'm gonna be with this team a good long time to come. I got no idea of being sent down like all the other rookies. I'm here to stay."

"What makes you so sure you'll make it?"

"I've been watching the rookies. I got 'em all beat by a mile. One day, kid, maybe you'll be sort of proud to tell your kids you once tried out with me."

"I hope you make it. But I sure won't—not this year. I'm too green, and I know it. But I'm sure in for a good time up here. Wait till I tell the gang back in Commerce I had a personal talk with Jolting Joe Di-Maggio."

Then, after he'd been in the camp for a few days, the press discovered him. "Where on earth did you learn to hit a ball like that?" one reporter asked him.

"My dad taught me. He started teaching me when I was just a little kid. I was about six when Dad and Gramps first taught me about switch-hitting. They had me practicing all the time."

"Oh, one of those fresh rookie kids," said the reporter. Long ago he had learned to divide the rookies into several types. Each year there were a few know-it-alls. The reporter disliked them most. He also noted that the smart alecks practically never made good.

"I really mean it," said Mickey. "Everyone in Commerce knows about it."

A few days later, when Mickey's drives were becoming the talk of the camp, the reporters found themselves spending a lot of time comparing notes on the young rookie from Oklahoma.

"It beats me," said sports editor Max Kase, "how a kid who can hit like that can be so modest. But it's no act. I thought it was at first. But no, he's on the level. He says he's too raw yet to even hope about them bringing him up this year. Says he hopes they send him to Kansas City. You know, I think he's the only rookie up here who hopes he'll get sent down.

"Just let him keep banging them the way we've

been seeing him do, and it's the Yankee Stadium for him, no matter what he wants."

Mickey was thrilled when he first found out that the reporters were mentioning him in their dispatches. Even if he flopped now, he told himself, he'd have those clippings. He'd read them all winter and he'd keep hoping for another chance. What a thrill to see his name in big-city papers!

And what nice guys the Yankees were! He'd never forget his first meeting with Joe DiMaggio.

"Hi, Mickey," Joe had said. "You sure hit a long one."

"You're the greatest," Mickey had answered, shyly. "I hope I someday get to be half as good as you."

"Don't sell yourself short," DiMaggio told him, giving him a friendly poke.

No, Mickey told himself. He'd never forget Phoenix. No matter what happened! He would never forget how wonderful the great Tommy Henrich was to him, showing him how to play the field and giving him helpful batting hints. And Joe DiMaggio helped too, and Phil Rizzuto, Eddie Lopat, Hank Bauer. It was the greatest thrill in the world to play alongside those stars. He would never forget those first weeks at Phoenix!

And then the pressure started to build. The newspaper raves became wilder and wilder. He was being mentioned now as the "rookie of the year." Then, as if that wasn't enough, it became "rookie of the ages."

"They're kidding," he kept telling himself as he read through some stories. "I never even played one big-league game yet. Besides, Casey knows I'm green. I'm dead sure to spend this season in the minors."

But he became less sure when the papers suddenly became full of praise from professional baseball men that was no different from what the reporters had said.

Casey himself told the press that he had never seen a rookie more promising than Mickey Mantle! Joe DiMaggio told one and all that there was no reason why Mickey couldn't develop into another Jolting Joe!

Without realizing it at first, Mickey began to tighten up. He began to feel the pressure.

Casey Stengel, with his sharp baseball eyes, was the first one to notice it. "Boy," he told Mickey one day, "I sure hope you ain't takin' in all that guff the press fellas are slingin' out about you. If you're readin' it, it's sure to ruin your eyesight."

Joe DiMaggio also noticed. "Mickey," he said one afternoon in the locker room, "I'll give you a little advice from one player to another. Take it easy. In this game, you got to learn to take it easy. Now, you know, the average fella back home thinks it's good to get your name in the paper every day. Well, it's nice, all right—once you get used to it. But it takes a heck of a lot of getting used to. You got to learn to roll with it. I had to learn. We all do. You got to make believe to yourself all the clapping is for some other guy. Start paying attention and, first thing, your mind is not on the game. Just keep your eye on the ball. You'll learn that's what really counts in baseball."

Then an incident took place that proved to Mickey just how green he was, and he became certain that he would not make the team. He was playing center field under the watchful eye of coach Tommy Henrich. Henrich, a great Yankee star for ten years, had been assigned the job of teaching the sensational rookie the mechanics of outfield play. Then, as a long drive was hit to Mantle, Henrich shouted directions. "Get it, Mickey. Don't go in too fast. Nice and easy. Judge the ball."

Mickey tore after the ball, misjudged it completely and almost fell down in embarrassment as the ball bounced off his shoulders. The trouble was that he had been wearing sunglasses attached to his cap for the first time, and he hadn't known how to flip the glasses a split second before the catch. Henrich consoled the youngster and taught him how to flip the glasses back over his cap, and he watched Mantle practice the move over and over.

The sportswriters observed the incident and got a big howl out of it. But they didn't place too much importance on it.

"After all," said one of them, "there are plenty of kids around who know how to fiddle with sunglasses like a real pro, but they couldn't hit a watermelon if it came floating over the plate. Mickey is slamming homers. So what difference does it make if he knows how to handle glasses or not? He'll learn."

That was it: "He'll learn." No one who watched Mickey doubted for a second that he'd learn. But it takes time to learn. And time was the one thing Mickey didn't have. Things were moving so fast for him.

Just two years before, he'd been a high-school student. Now, before he had even played a single big-league game, he was a household name—a name spoken in the same breath with that of Joe DiMaggio.

The strain became tremendous, and it kept getting bigger as the headlines became bigger. Each passing day, as the exhibition season rolled closer to an end, found Mickey more and more tense and jittery.

The day came when Casey announced that he was going to New York with the team. Then, before he knew it, he was speeding toward the big city.

"I must make it," he told himself as he rolled closer and closer to the Stadium in which he would have to prove himself. "Everyone is counting on me," he kept repeating to himself over and again.

Mickey knew that Mutt had been waiting for this since the day his son was born. Gramps had always told him that one day he'd make it. Then there were all the friends who had helped him—Barney Baxter, Ken Jacobson, Johnny Lingo, so many friends! There were the Commerce gang and the kids he'd gone to school with.

If I don't make good, he kept thinking, I won't be able to face anyone. Also there was the fact that he wanted to make good for himself. Isn't this what I've been aiming for all my life? If I flunk out, it's back to the mines. I mustn't goof this big chance.

When he arrived in New York, his stomach was in

knots again. He couldn't sleep a wink and walked the floor of the big New York hotel all through the long, black night.

In a way he was glad to see the morning sun rise, and he quickly packed his uniform in a bag and left for the big spacious ball park of the Yankees.

The big moment was finally here. It was now or never.

9.

"WHAT'S eatin' you, kid?" Yogi Berra asked Mickey. Berra was sprawled out on a bench in the locker room looking through a week-old Sunday newspaper's comic section.

"I just couldn't get any sleep last night," Mickey said. "I kept tossing this way and that way for a good position, but I just couldn't find it. I don't know how much shut-eye I actually got, but if it was more than a half hour I'd be amazed."

"That's right," Berra said. "It's your first big-league game out there today, ain't it? You were doin' so good during the exhibitions, I plumb forgot you're a rookie on the green side. So you got yourself first-game jitters, huh?"

"I don't mind telling you I'm a little scared to go out there at all."

Berra laughed. "It's the same for everybody. At least you don't look to me like you're ready to pass out and conk your head on the floor. I've seen rookies look kinda green around the eyes before walking out to that field for the first time."

Mickey stared out into space. "You know, so many years I waited for this. Sometimes I told myself I wasn't getting anywhere at all in baseball, and I'd never live to see the day when I'd walk out on the Yankee Stadium field. Now here it is and, Yogi, I just ain't ready."

"You look ready enough to me," the catcher said. "Stand up straight, let's take a good gander at you."

Mickey pulled himself erect.

"You look like you was born in that outfit, boy," Berra said. "Never seen a Yank look better in it. What's your number there? Seven, huh? Lucky seven! Good number! Now all you got to do is go out there and slug them balls like you've been sluggin' 'em, and you'll own yourself a famous number there."

"I wish I got some sleep," Mickey told him. "I always sleep sound as a mackerel. I just lay my head down and, bang! Next thing I know, it's time to get up and finish off breakfast. But last night, wow! Jitters all night!"

"Look at it this way," Berra said, holding up a page of the comics. "Look what this Superman fella got on his hands. He got a guy blastin' him with a powerful rocket gun that got atomic dust and hydrogen steam mixed in it. And it ain't only one guy out to get him. They got a whole army there of guys with stuff they ain't even invented yet, ready to blow him right into the next ten centuries. You think all of 'em put together can keep our boy Supe awake? Shows up each week in the Sunday papers lookin' like he spent the week in Miami takin' himself a tan and watchin' them bathin' beauties stroll by. Boy, all you got to do is get yourself a piece of a ball or two out there!"

"I'm not Superman, but I'll sure be trying."

After that, other Yank veterans stopped by to give him a word of encouragement. Casey said, "Stop lookin' like you swallowed yourself a watermelon in one gulp. You got yourself a great season comin' up."

Then Joe DiMaggio told him, "I know just how you're feeling before you walk out there. I owned plenty of goose-pimples myself that first time. But I'll tell you this. When I got that Yankee suit on for the first time, I felt like I suddenly shot up to twelve feet high. It's a powerful feeling. I just stood around wearing it, and I kept thinking of all those great players that wore that same suit. It sort of makes you feel, all by itself, that you're ready to go out there and play bang-up ball. Boy, it's great to be a Yank!"

"Sure is!" said Mickey, who appreciated Joe's words. But he still felt nervous.

"Time to go, everybody!" Casey suddenly yelled out. "They got cash customers waitin' for us out there!"

As Mickey walked through the tunnel that connects the Yankee dressing room with the field, he saw someone wave to him. It was Mutt! His father had stepped in to wish him luck.

"Mick," Mutt said, "we're all sittin' out there ready to cheer the walls down when you get yourself that first base hit today. What a day! The whole Commerce gang's sittin' there. They just can't wait for this game to start. Those who couldn't come up here with us, why they've been callin' me and droppin' me a line. You got a lot of friends rooting for you, Mickey. You got a couple of tons of 'em. Now you just remember not to get yourself too tense. Just make believe it's any old game, same as you been playin' all your life. And when those walls start tumblin' down, you know it's me and the whole Commerce gang yellin' our heads off for you."

"Thanks, Dad. Tell them all I sure appreciate their coming so far to see my first game."

"Now I don't want to hold you up any longer. You got a game to play out there, son. We can talk all we want after the game's over. But you got to get out there now. New York's waitin' for you!"

Now it was time to play ball!

"Here it comes," Mickey told himself, and he tried to get rid of the restless feeling that had taken hold of him. But he knew he was still more nervous than he had ever been before.

Vic Raschi was on the rubber for the Yanks, and the Red Sox had sent in Bill Wight, a recent acquisition, to oppose him.

When Mickey stepped up to bat in the first, he got a tremendous hand. The fans were seeing him for the first time, but there wasn't one that hadn't heard of him. His exploits in the training camp and on the exhibition tour had been publicized to baseball fans the world over.

"Hit it out of the park, Mickey!" the fans roared. This was what they expected of the rookie. Not a *hit,* but a *homer!* It wasn't realistic and it rattled Mickey.

He dug in with his spikes and waited for that first pitch to come. But when it came, it whizzed right past him. He was so jittery that he hadn't even seen the pitch. He took a deep breath to steady his nerves, wiped the perspiration away from his eyes, then stepped into the batter's box again.

He took a terrific cut at the next pitch, but he knew that it wasn't much of a hit. The bat had broken and the ball traveled slowly out to the infield. Mickey, fast as he was, hadn't been able to get anywhere near first before he was thrown out.

By the time he came up in the third, he was feeling a little better. Both Raschi and Wight were pitching tight ball. The only Yankee to really get a solid hit had been Jackie Jensen, who had taken over Hank Bauer's left-field job for the day. At the start of the third, Jensen had socked a long homer into the right-field stand with one on and had sent the Yanks ahead 2–0.

Now Mickey stepped up with the crowd's cheers for Jensen's blast still filling the air. "Hit, Mickey, hit!" they were yelling.

Mickey waited for Wight to give him one he could hit, and then lost patience. He took a cut at a bad ball and it went shooting high up into the air. It was an easy out for Vern Stephens playing third base for the Red Sox.

"I can't hit!" Mickey told Casey as he walked back to the dugout. "A weak smack and a little pop-up. That Wight is too smart for me!"

Casey smiled. "Mickey, you got a long way to go," he said. "Take a look at all of them great players. There's DiMaggio, and Mize, and Berra, and plenty of others. You think they all get themselves hits every time they come up. You think they kick this whole dugout in when they can't get on. Fella, not you and nobody else can get themselves on base all the time. You just settle yourself down a little and you'll get yourself on quick enough."

In the sixth, Jensen—who was clearly the hero of the day—led off with a savage two-bagger smash.

"This is my chance!" Mickey told himself as he faced Wight for the third time. "Now if I could only get a hit, I could send a man home. I got to pick out that curve ball. I've been watching for it, and if I get it. . . ."

The minute his bat connected with the ball he knew that he had just got his first big-league hit. The ball went shooting between short and third, and Jensen galloped home.

Standing on first, Mickey said, "I did it!"

"You sure did," said the Red Sox first baseman glumly.

That was the break the Yanks needed. DiMaggio, who followed Mantle, blasted a single, and so did Yogi Berra. This burst of hits, aided by a Bo-Sox error, sent three runs scampering over the plate and sent Bill Wight to the showers. Raschi continued to pitch shutout ball and held the Sox down to six hits, all singles, spread out over as many innings. The Yanks walked away with the game 5–0.

"Didn't I tell you you'd get yourself a hit?" said Casey to Mickey. "Whatcha worryin' about?"

Then Mutt and the Commerce gang congratulated Mickey on having successfully got through that first, tough one as a big-leaguer. "The rest'll be a lot easier," they told him. "The first of anything is always the hardest."

Mickey was still a little shaken when that day was over, but he was happy. Boy, it had felt good to get that hit and send Jensen across! If he had been able to get through that day, he felt, he could get through anything.

"No matter what happens to me in the future," he told his Commerce pals, "I'll never forget today." And then, when it came time to turn in, he slipped under the cover and slept as peacefully as a baby.

He was a big-leaguer now.

10.

NEW YORK CITY thrilled Mickey. But it also confused and even scared him more than a little.

The apartment he shared with his teammates, Hank Bauer and Johnny Hopp, was right smack in the middle of Times Square, the famous "Crossroads of the World." Each day more people passed through its streets than lived in the entire state of Oklahoma, let alone the town of Commerce.

"I can't really get over it," he kept telling Bauer and Hopp. "Back home we got only one movie house. If you don't like the picture, you stay home. But right here we got ourselves the pick of a dozen, or even more, movie houses without needing to walk more than a couple of blocks any-which way. Believe you me, I'm not gonna sit home looking out this apartment window when I got free time. I'm gonna see me a whale of a lot of pictures this season. I sure am gonna see all the cowboy pictures in town."

"Wanna bet?" said Bauer. "Time on your hands! Boy, you're a Yank now. Before the season's through, you'll feel yourself a heck of a lot more dried out than if you had one of those easy-going jobs lazying around in those cool mines."

Playing day after day with the world champ Yanks gave Mickey a thrill that hit him anew every time he walked out of the dugout. Every time he got settled in right field, he told himself how lucky he was. Why, he would think, Mickey, you ought to be somewhere up there in the stands hoping that some nice player will scribble his name for you on a piece of paper after the game. And here were kids all over the place asking every day for his autograph!

"What do I like best about being a Yank?" he said to a reporter. "Well, don't laugh your head off at me, but wow! there's so much special up here."

"Like what?"

"Like eating! Sure, I know all the fellas get a laugh when I tell them I'm hungry all the time. But I've never had steaks like these every day. Casey told me that I could eat all I want. So I guess I'm eating all the time I'm not playing. And, you know, I ain't been hungry up here like I used to be plenty times in Joplin. I sure like the eating up here. I can tell you that.

"Then I got to tell you about the bats. I guess the thing that surprises me is that every player has half a dozen of his own bats. All the players have their favorites. But down in Joplin we had only two bats. One was a Chuck Klein bat, and the other was a Harry Craft, named by the bat people after our manager. I guess we didn't know better, and I guess the team couldn't afford to buy more than two bats at a time. When one bat broke, Harry would send a boy down to the store to buy us a new one."

The little things caught his eye—the comfort and

style of the big league. And every day the thrill kept getting bigger. Mickey was sure he'd never get used to being a Yank.

And the tension boiling in him was still there. It had been building up. The fans, who knew his press raves by heart, wanted him to sock one out of the park every time he came up to hit. The reporters, knowing that he was good copy and knowing what he could do when he broke loose, poured on the publicity.

Now he was pressing, trying to hit the big homer every time, and he began to swing at pitches that he couldn't have reached with a ten-foot pole. He was a sucker for every sharp-breaking curve that came his way, and he kept piling up the strike-outs. "I can't tell you what it is," he told Casey. "I'm darned if I got any idea myself. I just keep swinging and missing. It must be the pitchers. They really know all the tricks up here. And I still don't. I guess that's it."

"Nothin' wrong with the kind of thinkin' you're doin'," Casey answered. "Sure, these here pitchers got all that stuff on the ball. You think they let 'em get on that mound out there 'cause of their good looks? Most of 'em are pretty smart fellas. Sure, they got themselves ten tricks to your one. They been up here longer. Now if you'll just stop trying to knock every ball out of the park, just because the sports writers want to have something new to write about, why then you might start hitting. Just meet the pitch squarely. Timing is the whole answer to good solid hitting. Just meet the ball. Hit it to the infield, then after a spell, when your swing is back in a groove, you'll hit the long ones over the fence."

But Casey's pep talk and pointers didn't do the trick. Mickey was pressing too hard, and the pitchers had his number. They were throwing to his weak spot. Every ball pitched to him was low and tight, right on his hands, and he was helpless.

"Casey, I got no confidence up there any more. I thought I could hit every pitcher that ever lived, but I never saw pitchers like these. They got me all figured out on the mound out there. I tell you they save up their best sucker throws for me. They don't waste them on nobody else."

"It takes a fella a little time to learn," Casey said. "You think DiMaggio knew the whole works first time he laid his eyes on a pitcher in the majors?"

"I'm no Joe DiMaggio."

"You'll be pickin' up. They charge for learnin' up here. You're paying 'em with three strikes—like buyin' a house for a buck a week or somethin'."

At times Mickey felt that he was improving. The second time he faced a pitcher he hit him better than during his first try. But the strike-outs still came, as he put it, "with sickening steadiness," and he lost control altogether.

Finally, in the second week of July, Casey called him in for a private talk.

"Boy," he said, "I think just the same about you as before. You got tremendous ability. You remember the game when we had the A's tryin' to kill us off. You got five solid drives that day. Three out of five when

Lou Brissie pitched against us. Then you walloped two more higher'n Hank Wyse could see when he tried to zing 'em past you in the second. That's Mickey Mantle out there, I told 'em all on the bench. One of my boys. Got a big career comin' up for him! And he's just a young one."

Mickey didn't say a word. His heart was thumping, and he knew what was coming.

"It's just," Casey continued, "you got yourself so ragged dancin' yourself around in circles, you're swingin' even before them bad pitches come over. Oh, I been keeping an eye on you. I been seein' you ruinin' all those benches in the locker kicking them around. But in the big leagues, son, you got to act like a big-leaguer, not like some little high-school kid. You're not doin' yourself or the ball club any good, the way you're strikin' out."

"You're sending me down?"

"Yes, Mickey, I'm sendin' you down to Kansas City. You'll play regular there, and I'm sure you're gonna be back with us in a hurry. Keep those strike-outs down, and remember you're on a twenty-four-hour recall."

As Mickey walked out of Casey's office, he felt as if he'd just died—as if his feet were lugging a corpse around. Sure, he figured, Casey had been kind and gentle with him. Casey was that kind of guy. But the handwriting had been on the wall, and now the ax had fallen.

Mickey, he told himself, you're through in big-league baseball. They'll never bring you up again.

All those years of hoping and playing and praying—it was for nothing at all. Maybe it would have been better, he thought, if he'd just gone on playing with local teams until his time came to go into the mines.

He had no complaints. He knew that Casey had given him as fair and square a chance as anyone had ever got from any major-league manager. He'd kept him in the lineup as long as he could. But there was a limit to everything.

In his first 246 times at bat for the Yanks, Mickey had struck out 52 times! He had no one to blame but himself. He felt as if he had lost everything. He just was glad that he didn't have to see his friends from Commerce. He couldn't face them. He couldn't face anyone now. Not even Mutt. He couldn't stand tearing his heart out with the bad news.

On July 15 the story that Mickey was being sent down hit the papers. It caused a sensation among fans everywhere, and the reporters mobbed around Casey for details.

"Does this mean that Mantle's through?" they asked him.

"You wish you was through like that kid's through," snapped Casey.

"We know you're a loyal guy, Casey. We know you wouldn't want to do damage to the kid's spirit by saying that he turned out to be a busher. But what's the low-down?"

Casey looked that particular reporter right in the eye. "The kid's as good as they come and make you no mistake about that."

Then he addressed the reporters as a group: "Fellas, the kid came up to us from 'way down there with a tag on him he's a shortstop. Well, he belongs out there in the field with DiMag, and we put him there. Right away, overnight, he's a kid you can see learns one-two-three. He runs, fields, throws. He hits a ball long as a ball can go. He clouts that ball right, he smacks it left. Everything!"

"Then how come you sent him down?"

"Just one little bad thing he did. He struck out too much. That's no good. It don't matter that he hits those long homers. He can't keep his average up when he's strikin' out all the time. But bend your ears to this. He needs a little more help in Kansas City. That's all. They got orders to play him in center field every game. Every day. And we also got him on twenty-four-hour option. Let him hit like I know he can and I'll have him back here with me overnight. That's the way it has to be. Mickey has to hit his way back. I know he can do it."

The result of this interview was that the next day's stories in the papers seemed unusual in a way. First, they announced that the Yanks were bringing up Art Schallock, a sensational young pitcher from the West Coast, and that Mantle had to be sent down to allow the Yanks to keep within the player limit. Then, after quoting Casey on Mantle's too many strike-outs, they quoted him as saying that Kansas City had orders to play him every day in center field. Why center field? the reporters wondered. He had played right field in the Stadium. The answer was obvious: He was being groomed to replace Jolting Joe in center field next season.

Never before had a player, at the very moment that he was being sent down from the majors, been spoken of as the next season's replacement for one of the greatest players in all history!

But all this went over Mickey's head. He was too downhearted to wonder about whether Casey had really meant 'it when he told him that he would be brought up again if his hitting improved. In Mickey's mind, he was through.

And his playing at Kansas City showed just how defeated he felt. His heart just wasn't in the games he played. His manager, the former Yankee outfielder "Twinkletoes" Selkirk, who took right field over from Babe Ruth some eighteen years earlier, heaped on the encouragement. He kept telling Mickey that a good season with K.C. would land him right back with the Yanks. But he couldn't get it across to the downcast young player.

In his first ten games with Kansas City, Mickey didn't get a single hit!

Then Mutt Mantle came to town. He listened while Mickey sobbed out the story to him. He made no effort to console his son. To Mickey's amazement, he talked to him in a tone he had never heard before. A real tough man-to-man tone.

"Now I've heard everything you got to say, Mickey. And I didn't say one darn thing. Oh, I could've said a whole lot you wouldn't've liked to hear. But I kept my mouth shut. And now I'm giving it to you."

Mickey stared at his father.

"What the heck do you think?" said Mutt, raising his voice. "That you're still six years old? You're a man now and you're out in the world. It's a hard world with no soft cushions for the losers and the crybabies! You go for something and don't make it—bang! You land right on your head! You don't get nothing without fighting for it. They kick you down, you do your darn best to drag yourself up. So you been taking a licking! What the heck do you think it's like down in those mines for your whole life! If all you can do about your licking is sit around and feel sorry for yourself, then pack up and let's get out of here. You'll sign up in the mines and spend the next sixty years down there!"

"What do you want me to do, Dad?"

"I want you to get out on that field and fight your fool head off! If you still can't do it, okay. We'll say you flopped fair and square. You tried your best. But don't give me this crybaby I'm-washed-up-at-nineteen stuff."

The change in Mickey was almost miraculous. Overnight, he started belting the ball left and right. The fans in K.C. got used to saying, "Here comes another Mantle extra-baser!" Or, "Another ball lost!"

"Twinkletoes" Selkirk was as delighted as the fans. "Kid," he'd say to Mickey, "just don't press too much. Don't forget to pick out those good pitches. Make those pitchers pitch to you the kind of ball you want. Wait 'em out, they've got to come in with a fat pitch. When they do, just meet the ball."

Mickey followed Selkirk's sound advice. He waited and waited for the big pitches, then drove the ball out of the park. Now he was in the groove again and cutting down his strike-outs.

Mickey stayed in K.C. only forty-six days. He was hitting .361 and had slammed out eleven home runs when the Yanks sent him a hurry-back-home call late in August.

Back in the Stadium, Mickey was just what the Yankees needed. They were in second place, three games behind the Indians, when Mickey put on his Number 7 uniform again. His long and timely hits drove enemy pitchers to cover, and his great play sparked the entire ball club. By September 1 the Yanks were back in first place again, and after that it was no race. Casey's boys copped their third straight pennant.

The miracle Yankee team under the Old Professor had held together once more. Joe DiMaggio had inspired the ball club and played like a demon in spite of his bad heels. And a nineteen-year-old kid from Commerce, Oklahoma, named Mantle had come back from Kansas City to stand alongside of DiMaggio with his big home-run bat to cinch a pennant for the Yankees.

And then the zigzagging Mantle luck zigzagged again. His luck broke in front of 66,018 goggle-eyed fans.

It happened during the fifth inning of the second game of the World Series. Willie Mays slugged a zooming drive to right center, and Mantle and DiMaggio raced for the ball. Then, suddenly, Mickey crashed to the ground. He didn't trip or stumble or go down on one knee. He pitched over on his face and lay motionless on the ground.

The huge crowd was suddenly on its feet. What had happened to Mantle? Speculation ran riot. Had he had a heart attack? He hadn't fallen. He had collapsed! Joe DiMaggio played it easily. As Mantle collapsed, Joe grabbed the ball and returned it to the infield. Then he motioned for help and flopped down beside Mickey. He did all three things so smoothly that it was almost as if he had done them in one motion.

"What happened, kid? Mickey, what happened?"

Mickey's answer was a moan, and then the stretcher came and carried him into the dressing room.

When he came to, he wasn't able to say what had happened. One minute he'd been running after the ball and then, without warning, he felt as if he had no legs. Now he felt this unbearable pain in his left knee.

"It's a bad one. You stepped onto a drainpipe in the field, and your knee conked out," the doc told him. "You're through with baseball for the rest of the year, Mickey."

Mickey lay there in pain thinking everything had been for nothing. He thought about how some fans talked about his "luck." *Luck!* All that work since he was a kid. The superhuman effort it had taken to drag himself back to the team after his talk with Mutt in Kansas City.

This time he had really had it. What major-league team would want a guy with injuries in both legs? A player whose legs had to be bandaged before and after every game?

He wished Mutt were there. He wanted to tell him that he had tried his very best. But it was no good. "Lucky" Mickey Mantle had no luck at all.

11.

"HI, DAD. It's like old times again, ain't it, with me laying around in the hospital all tied up with bandages?" Mickey said as Mutt walked into the room.

"How much is it hurting?"

"It's not too bad." Then the pain shot through his knee and Mickey groaned out loud. "Anyway," he added when the pain eased up, "it's a heck of a lot better than yesterday. I thought for a time they wanted to cut the leg off. They kept giving me all kinds of shots to get the pain down, but nothing helped."

"I was just listening to the doc," Mutt told him. "No kidding you, son, about that leg. The doc will be in to tell you about it soon, anyway. You just about ripped every ligament you got there. The knee is going to give you a lot of trouble for a long time, and it may never heal properly. I don't know how much ball you're gonna play, son. Only time will tell."

Mickey's smile froze. He turned his face to the wall. "I know, Dad," he said. "Nobody's got to tell me. The hurt in that knee tells me the whole story."

"But," said Mutt, brightening up, "the doc also says you could be back in there next season if we're lucky and it heals okay."

"You tell him," Mickey said angrily, turning to face Mutt, "there ain't no ifs about it. I'm gonna play if I have to go up there and hit on one leg. I mean it, Pop. Nobody's gonna stop me now. I'm a Yankee."

Mutt laughed. "You'll be all right, Mick. When I see you with all that fight, I stop worrying."

"Anyway," answered Mickey, relaxing, "I got a little luck."

"How so?"

"There's nobody in this room with me," he said. "That bed there's empty. They're bringing me in a TV set later, so I can watch the game today. I'd go nuts if one of those wise guys was in the other bed talking through the whole game."

"You got a big surprise coming up for you, fella," said Mutt.

And then the surprise came. An interne came in, carrying hospital clothes.

"You can change here, Mr. Mantle," he said to Mutt. "Just leave your clothes on the chair and a nurse will pick them up. I'll be back later to look in on you."

"What's up?" Mickey said after the interne left. "Gosh, you moving in here with me?

"No kidding, what is it, Dad?" He took a long look at Mutt and then for the first time noticed how pale his father looked.

"Well, it's that miserable back of mine. It's acting up again a little. Nothing much to lose sleep about, but I figured I might as well have the doctors look at it. Besides, we can watch the game together."

Mickey was greatly relieved. He had begun to

think that Mutt was really sick. He did look tired, and worried.

So they lay there in adjoining beds and watched TV. And the fact that the Yanks swept to their third world championship in a row did them both more good than medicine. They both nearly jumped out of bed cheering when the Giants were beaten into the ground in six exciting games. And in short order both Mantles, father and son, were on the train racing for home.

Back home in Commerce, Mickey went through an agonizing winter. For most of the time, the leg was useless to him. He dragged himself around in a brace and was very depressed by the time the doctor decided that he could get along with just a weighted boot.

"It's a pleasure not to have to drag around that brace," Mickey said. "But how the heck will I be able to play with that heavy boot?"

"You'll be able to take it off by the opening game," Mutt answered. "Just keep exercising those muscles. Keep them in shape, and you'll be ready. Now don't fuss."

By the time Mickey reported to training camp the boot was off. But he still had to have the leg bandaged before and after every game. The important thing, however, was that he could run. He tried not to worry but sometimes he suddenly found himself limping and hurting badly.

It was a downcast camp that he reported to. All the players were in the dumps and Casey didn't look his usual chipper self.

"Casey's had three miracles in a row," the reporters

were saying. "But he'll be pushing his luck too far if he tries for a fourth pennant. Not this year. He doesn't have a ghost of a chance."

Nobody had to spell out why the Yank chances looked so slim. But the press spelled it out, anyway, in dispatch after dispatch. Big Joe DiMaggio had finally hung up his spikes. One of the greatest stars of all time, DiMaggio had finally decided that he couldn't face another season of agonizing injuries. There were other problems with the club. Pitcher Tom Morgan and second baseman Gerry Coleman were in the armed forces, and Bobby Brown, a fine utility player, would be called up soon. Mickey Mantle was hobbling around the training camp like a kid learning to walk, and there were at least six other players hurting.

"You know," said one reporter, "the Yanks this year look like the Confederate armies after the last battle of the Civil War."

Plainly, it would be a miracle if Casey could win a pennant with this harried-looking bunch of Yankee ballplayers.

"Listen," Casey told the press, "I told you a hundred times already I still ain't got no idea. Sure, *somebody* will replace DiMaggio in center field, but don't ask me who. I still ain't got no idea."

That hole in center field was the biggest immediate problem facing the Yanks. And it looked as if the problem would get bigger and bigger as the season went on.

One thing Mickey was sure of: he wouldn't play it. How could Casey send a player who was limping out there to cover that rolling territory? The thought that he wouldn't get to take over DiMaggio's old spot ate away at Mickey's insides. He'd been aiming at that position from the minute that he first signed a Yankee contract.

"I don't care where I play," he finally decided. "Just so long as they play me. I'll go nuts if this trick knee benches me."

Mickey opened the season in right field. Trick knee or not, he decided that he had to get off to a fast start. He wanted that center-field spot, and the only way that he could show Casey how he felt was to get off fast and running. He did just that in the opening game of the season against the Athletics' pitcher Carl Sheif. Mickey slammed out three solid base hits and fielded his position well, and he continued his great play during the early weeks of the season. "Keep this up," he said to himself, "and Casey will have to put me in DiMag's old position."

And then Mickey, who had already got more than his share of the bad breaks, received the worst news of his life.

Mutt Mantle was dead! It had been cancer. Mickey's mother had wanted to tell him, but Mutt had told her not to. "Why worry the kid?" he'd said. "He can't do nothing about it. Nobody can. And it'll ruin his playing. Let's spare him all the worry."

Mutt was a young man when he died. Only forty. But he had seen his dream come true. He had seen his son make the big leagues and win a permanent spot on the Yanks. He had also seen Mickey play in the World Series.

"Momma," Mutt had said to his wife, "I guess now Mutt Mantle has seen everything."

Mickey went home and heard the whole story from his mother. He stood pale and shaken when they put Mutt into the ground. Then, between tears, he said softly to himself, "So long, Dad. I'll be thinking about you every day of my whole life. You were always the greatest. I'll never forget how you sacrificed everything for me and the rest of the kids. Now, I'm responsible for the family. I'll take over, Pop," he whispered softly.

Mutt was gone. Gramps was gone. The two men who had made him into a ballplayer were no more.

I'll never let them down, Mickey vowed to himself on the ride back to New York.

He found the Yanks a discouraged ball club when he reached Yankee Stadium. They weren't winning games, and had no spirit or hustle. No talk about winning another pennant. No talk about playing in the World Series. Casey was wearing a long face. He kept shifting the team around almost daily. But nothing worked.

Then Mantle reported back in action and suddenly the team caught fire. Mickey was furnishing the spark and the whole team was digging in and playing better ball. Cleveland and Boston were fighting for the league leadership, but now in June the Yanks started to move.

"C'mon!" Casey was now yelling to them from the dugout. "We got only half a season to go. Let's go! Let's run! Come on, boys! Come on, Mickey!"

Mickey was hitting the ball well and slashing long

drives when they counted most. He won game after game with booming hits.

"What a slam!" Casey said to him one day. "What a hit! The way that there apple rammed itself up against that top tier of Briggs Stadium, I thought the whole stand would flop down!"

"Thanks, Casey," Mickey said.

"Ha!" Casey said. "Didja hear that, everybody! The boy's thankin' me. For what? Old Casey didn't belt that apple." He bowed to Mickey from the waist in his famous dramatic style. "I thank *you*, fella!"

Casey was watching a new Mickey Mantle. Mickey had returned to the team with a purpose. He was more determined now. He was serious. He didn't horse around on the field. He was in deadly earnest and played every hit for that extra base. He was now the man of the Mantle family and he had a family to care for. He had to be in the game every day.

There was the day when a sharp drive came bouncing out to Mickey, who was now playing in Joe Di-Maggio's center-field spot. The Tigers had a man on second, who was off and running with the hit. Mickey scooped up the ball and fired it to the plate in one effortless motion, and the runner was out at the plate. The crowd roared at Mickey's great peg, and he doffed his cap in acknowledgment of the tribute.

"Did you see that!"

The fans were on their feet and roaring. It had been one of those great throws that a fan sees two or three times a season.

The Yanks in the dugout clapped each other on the

back. "Jumping Jupiter! It came across like a shot from a cannon!"

But Casey wasn't yelling. He wasn't even smiling.

When Mickey came off the field, he said to Casey, "It was a hard play to make. It ended lucky. The guy could have scored, but I felt sure that I could make a good throw and cut off a run."

It was only then that Casey smiled. "Mickey, that's big-league thinkin'. I was boilin' at you just a minute ago while all the fans were yellin' their mouths off. But now you're showin' me that you're startin' to think about certain plays. You just keep doin' that, son. Keep it up."

The season's finish was a thriller. Sparked by Mantle, the Yanks took game after game, winning fourteen of their last sixteen games!

On September 26, Casey's boys won their fourth pennant in a row!

It was a feat that only two other men had ever achieved. Joe McCarthy had won four pennants in a row for the Yanks. In the National League, only John McGraw had been able to pull off the trick. Now the Old Professor joined McCarthy and McGraw in the record books as one of the great all-time managers.

But Casey himself summed up the '52 race with one sentence: "That Mickey Mantle was the big difference for us. He picked up the team with his speed and big bat. Just like DiMaggio did the last couple of years."

Tributes to Mantle poured in from all sides. No one doubted that it had been Mantle who had kept the

Yanks in the running and had booted them home with his hustle and hitting.

He had hit twenty-three homers. He had jumped his batting average from .267 in his freshman year to .311, a whacking jump of forty-four points. He ended the season tied with George Kell of the Red Sox for third place in batting honors in the American League.

The experts no longer doubted that Mickey Mantle was a real big-leaguer. The press boys happily began to remind one and all that they had spotted Mantle as an outstanding player from the start. "Didn't we tell you so, 'way back in those first days in the Phoenix training camp?"

And so they had.

But the season wasn't really over yet. There was still a tough World Series ahead with the Dodgers. Could Mickey, with ligaments torn in one leg and osteomyelitis in the other, help the Yanks beat the powerful Dodger team?

All baseball fans waited for the answer.

12.

IN the 1952 Series the Dodgers were out for blood. Three years earlier they had grappled with Casey Stengel's Yankees for the world championship and had taken a humiliating beating, four games to one.

But this was a different Dodger team. They were a hard-hitting, slick-running ball club with plenty of good pitching and a brainy baseball strategist in Chuck Dressen, who was managing the Brooks.

"Don't go kiddin' yourself about them Dodgers," Casey told his team. "Beatin' them is gonna be some job. Look who they got out there. Jackie Robinson— he hits 'em in a pinch. Then there's Roy Campanella, and Newcombe, Gil Hodges and that Duke. These boys can hit the ball a mile."

The Old Professor cleared his throat. "If the Dodgers can't hit one out of the park fair and square, they'll run crazy on the bases. Robinson, Furillo, Reese—don'tcha dare take your eyes off them for even a tiny piece of a second! Fast! Like the wind, and they can get those big base hits when they need them."

"Casey, you trying to scare us?" said Yogi Berra.

"The Dodgers? You trying to scare us away from them. Sure they're pretty good, but we've got ourselves a couple of fair ballplayers, too. Remember?"

"Glad you're gettin' it, Yogi boy," Casey said. "At least a wee bit of a tiny part of it. I'm scarin' you, all right. We won three pennants in a row and everybody around here's beginning to talk like it's the easiest thing in the world to beat those Dodgers. You're too cocky and sure of yourselves. Now I want you to remember, those Brooklyn fellas are mean and smart and they hustle, and just one little slip-up, one messy play, and you can lose the Series. Now, just remember that."

Casey was taking no chances. Down in Ebbets Field he lined them all up against an outfield wall. "This here wall's new to plenty of you. You ever seen it before? Well, you just look it over. I want you should see how it's straight there, and how it goes out, and in. Take a good look. The balls angle off in all directions, and if you don't play the ball right, why, those Dodgers will run wild on you. I know how to play in this park. I played for this ball club a long time ago."

In the first game, Mantle smashed through for two long singles in four trips to the plate, as pitcher Joe Black completely thwarted the Yankees 4–2. The Yanks copped the second game 7–1. Mantle drove in two runs, slashed out three hits and stepped into the spotlight as the outstanding player of the Series. The Dodgers came back to wrap up the third game 5–3, but the Yankees behind Allie Reynolds' four-hit pitching stopped the Brooks cold with a 2–0 shutout. The Dodgers came storming back to snare the fifth game 6–5 in an eleven-inning thriller.

And there it stood—three games for the fire-eating Dodgers and only two for the sagging Yankees. One more would give the Dodgers the World Series.

"There's one thing I want you to know, Mickey." Casey sat down beside him. "You been playin' good ball. Great ball through the season, outstanding ball in this here Series. You came through for us when we needed you most, and I won't forget it."

"Ah, Casey," said Mickey, "how can anybody be playing good ball when they're leading us three games to two."

"Tomorrow you just watch us mop up that place with them. And the next day just the same way. Anybody thinks we ain't gonna take this here Series from them is gotta date with one of them head doctors. And you, Mickey," he said, sticking his finger into Mickey's chest, "are gonna carry this ball club just like Mister DiMaggio did. Now you know how much I'm countin' on you."

The next day manager Chuck Dressen sent Billy Loes out to end the Series. The Dodgers were so sure they were in, they could barely sit still in the dugout. All they had to do was take this game and that was the end of the Yankees. Just taking this game would do it.

They got off to a great start. In the sixth, Duke Snider broke a 0–0 tie with a tremendous homer.

Dressen's smile was so big you could practically see

it from the top of the grandstand. A vision of the world championship danced before his eyes. Three more scoreless innings for the Yanks and that was that.

But Berra blasted away Dressen's smile with a homer every bit as long as Snider's. A few plays later, Vic Raschi drove Woodling home from second. The Yanks were ahead 2–1. There was still fire in the champions' play.

Casey studied the situation. The one-run lead wasn't enough. He knew that. The Dodgers were booming with confidence. He knew that the Yankees needed something that would set them on fire. Something that would give them back their old hustle and let them go into the next day's game confident of victory.

The Old Professor danced out to speak to Mantle.

"Mickey," he said. "You're comin' up to bat now. This fella Black, out there pitchin' for Brooklyn, is a smart one. Now he knows a few things about pitchin', but I know a couple of things about him. He's got a good curve ball, and you look for it real good. When it comes in, hit it out of the park. Remember, boy, the curve ball, and bang it over the wall. Wait for the curve!"

Mickey tried to smile. "It's a big order."

"I'm talkin' to my big fella," said Casey. "Now go get yourself a bat."

Mickey, batting left-handed, let the first pitch go by. It was a curve ball and a beauty. "Strike one." Mickey set himself for the next pitch, hoping for the fast curve ball. It broke sharply as Mickey's big bat slashed at the pitch nervously. Whack! He caught the ball with the fat part of his bat and the ball took off as if jet-propelled. Higher and higher it went into the stands for a home run. The huge crowd thundered its approval as Mickey scampered around the bases to be greeted by the entire Yankee bench. It was the big hit of the Series and was the game for the Yanks. The Series was now tied 3–3.

The weather was near-perfect the next day, and the fans settled back for a pitcher's duel. Dressen sent Black in again, and Casey chose Ed Lopat to do the honors for the Yankees. But in the fourth inning the batters took over. Rizzuto doubled for the Bombers and Mize singled him home. The Dodgers answered by filling the bases. A sacrifice fly brought a run home for them. Then Gene Woodling blasted a homer in the fifth, putting the Yanks ahead 2–1, only to have the Dodgers come back and even things up.

And that was how things stood when Mantle came up in the sixth. A tie, with both teams beginning to break under the pressure.

"Another hit now or never!" Casey yelled from the dugout.

Mickey dug his spikes in and waited for the ball. Then he swung practically from the ground. The ball soared into the stands for another homer and the tie was broken.

The big blow just about broke the Dodgers' spirit. They knew that the Series was over when Mantle came up again and drove in the final run of the game with a single.

Casey raved about Mantle to the reporters who flooded into the locker room. "Didn't I tell all you fellas way back in Phoenix I got myself a little Melvin Ott here. What a ballplayer!"

Then he began to recall plays Mickey had made. "That fella Mantle's got the iron nerves of one of them burglar fellas! Imagine any fella with the nerve to drag-bunt with two strikes on him in a World Series. Oh, it was a little play, not so important as a homer. But it was *baseball*—real baseball. A perfect one-hundred-per-center of a bunt, too. I seen him do it seven, eight times just this season. Once against Cleveland he sees this here pitcher, see, rushin' in to field the ball. So what does he do? He switches and pushes it right towards their shortstop. Gets away with it, too. I tell you I ain't seen nothin' like it since Cobb himself!"

Jackie Robinson paid Mickey a tribute that ran in every sports section of the country:

"That boy Mantle is tremendous. He was the margin of victory for the Yankees, and the margin of defeat for us. Mantle was the only difference between the two clubs."

The statistics told the story of how Mickey had helped the Yankees in the Series: In seven games, he had batted .345, with ten hits, including two crucial homers, a triple and a double.

But the records couldn't tell the story of how much it had meant to the Yankee team's morale to have Mickey with them that year.

Even the great Rogers Hornsby, one of baseball's immortal Hall-of-Fame stars, was impressed. "No reason why that Mantle boy shouldn't develop some day into one of baseball's greatest all-time sluggers," he told the press.

But even though the praise was music to his ears, Mickey didn't tarry. He had other things on his mind.

For one thing, his home town of Commerce was preparing in his honor the biggest celebration it had ever held. It was to be called Mickey Mantle Day and the young player's friends, neighbors and fans from towns in three surrounding states were waiting for him to make a triumphant home-coming.

But the biggest thing on Mickey's mind was a bright-eyed, good-looking young girl named Merlyn Johnson.

She was his bride. Never was a young couple more head over heels in love, but the going had been rough for them in the less than a year that they had been married.

Mutt's death had hit Mickey very hard, and he'd been feeling far from his usual cheerful self. Also, he'd struggled to get his legs in shape and he'd been in physical pain much of the time. But the going had been much easier because Merlyn was at his side.

Then the season had begun and he had to leave her. He'd written every night and spent more than he could afford on long-distance calls every other day. But he'd missed her so much that there had been times when he could barely think of anything else.

And now the season was over and he was free to go home to Commerce.

In the Yankee locker room Phil Rizzuto, the great Yankee shortstop, was praising Mickey to the skies.

"Mickey, in all the years I've been with the ball club, I've never seen the kind of ball you showed us in this Series."

"Yeah," chirped in Yogi Berra with a grin a mile wide. "You hit that ball like a million."

"Never saw a youngster hit the ball as hard as you, and as consistently," said Gerry Coleman.

While all this praise filled the huge locker room at the Stadium and his teammates were thumping him on the back, offering their congratulations, Mickey's thoughts were far away.

Tomorrow, he thought—and his heart beat a little faster as he thought about it—tomorrow, this time, I'll be with Merl. He hurriedly jammed his uniform and baseball equipment in the huge Valpack, quickly shook hands with all of the players, jumped into his shining new blue Cadillac convertible and was off for Commerce and Merl.

13.

MICKEY had seen Merlyn Johnson for the first time during the winter after he graduated from high school. He'd been sitting around one afternoon watching a football game between Commerce and Picher high schools when he suddenly said to a friend:

"Just look at that girl on the field there! She sure is a beauty!"

The friend took a long look at Picher's drum majorette and whistled softly. "She sure is beautiful," he agreed.

"I wonder what she's like," Mickey said. He couldn't take his eyes off the girl.

"Just ask me," said a Picher student sitting next to him. "I know everybody at Picher."

"You know *her*?" Mickey asked.

"Everybody knows Merlyn Johnson," was the answer. "She's sort of a Picher celebrity, you could say. She's drum majorette of the school. She's also the soloist at the First Baptist Church over in Picher. Terrific voice."

"How does someone get to meet her?"

"She's a very friendly girl," said the Picher boy. "If

you talk to her I'm sure she'll say Hello before she walks away." Then he took a good look at Mickey. "But if you got any funny ideas in mind, you'd better forget all about them right now."

"I don't have any funny ideas in mind. It's just that she's so beautiful."

Later, Mickey got himself introduced when a group of boys and girls were standing around talking. He wanted to ask Merlyn for a date, but he lost his nerve.

Then, a little while later, Merlyn received a phone call in her home in Picher, which was only three miles from Commerce. It was one of her best friends. "Merl," she said, "there's a certain boy who thinks your looks make all the Hollywood stars look sick."

"And who may that be?" asked Merlyn.

"It's Mickey Mantle. You remember him, don't you? You were introduced to him after the football game with Commerce."

"Oh, yes," said Merlyn, who remembered the handsome young fellow who was supposed to be a baseball player. Merlyn was a football fan. She knew the game inside out. But she knew nothing about baseball. She didn't even know the rules of the game.

"Well, he asked me to call you up to see if you're willing to go out on a date with him."

"My answer is to ask you to go back and tell John Alden that Priscilla said for him to speak for himself. If he didn't sleep through his English class at Commerce, he'll know what I'm talking about."

Finally, they went out on a date with some other couples. Mickey hardly said anything at all. But when he returned home he raved to Mutt about the girl he'd met.

"Boy," said Mutt, "you sure sound like you got yourself a bad case of puppy love. I ain't heard no one talk sweet words like that about a girl since the day when I first met your ma. But I wasn't no puppy then, boy."

"It's more than just words, Dad. It's no case of puppy love, either. Someday I'm gonna marry that girl."

"There's nothing wrong in wanting to get married. But it's all the more reason why you should pay real attention to your baseball now. You want a wife, you got to be able to put a roof over her head and meat and potatoes on the table. You become a big-leaguer and then you won't just be talking. You'll be ready for a wife then."

As time passed, Mickey and Merl saw each other more and more often, and in time she became Mickey's steady girl. His parents liked her at once, and her family took to him, too. They were married after Mutt's death and set themselves up in a house of their own.

Mickey taught Merl the rules of baseball, and pretty soon she showed signs of becoming something of an expert.

"Now that's what I call *hitting*!" said Merlyn to her husband on Mickey Mantle Day in Commerce after he hit a homer out of the park in the big exhibition game.

Mickey had been managing and playing for Joplin, his old team, against the Boyer All-Stars. The game had been the high point of the big Commerce holiday in his honor.

Before game time, he'd been a little nervous. "Gosh," he said, to a group of fans. "What if I strike out four times in a row?"

"You won't," they roared.

He didn't. He rapped a sharp single, a tremendous double, and a homer that lost the ball.

It was like a scene out of a movie. Local boy makes good. Comes home to show his friends and neighbors how he did it. Plays the greatest ball that anyone in his town ever saw.

The day was one that no one in Commerce would forget for a long time to come. And neither would Mickey Mantle!

Best of all, he was home with Merl.

"We got all winter to ourselves," Mickey told her.

"I know," she said, her joy showing in her face. "But it's not enough. We have to be together all the time."

And then Mickey put his arms around her, lifted her off her feet, and told her the good news.

"I got a raise! Next year we're renting a house for ourselves near the Stadium. You're coming to New York with me and we'll be together all season!"

"Oh, Mickey, that's the best news yet," Merl said, throwing her arms around her beaming husband.

14.

"LET'S go out and get ourselves a fifth pennant in a row," said Casey in the spring of 1953. "There ain't no one can stop us."

Five in a row! Casey's four straight victories had already put him in the record books as one of baseball's all-time managers. Was he trying now to set records that no future manager would be able to break?

The 1953 season loomed as one of the most interesting in diamond history.

"You know," said one reporter, who had always been quick to downgrade Casey and talk about the Old Professor's luck, "I think maybe the old boy's headed for another win this year."

"Now that's what I call a real reckless guess," said another scribe sarcastically. "Is there anyone this year who don't feel Casey has the season in the bag?"

Actually, some reporters were by no means ready to concede that the season was a shoo-in for the Yanks. There were a lot of new players added to the other clubs, and baseball was still a game in which just about anything could happen. But it was interesting to note that, for the first time in five years, most of the reporters picked the Yanks.

In previous years the scribes had looked at the injury-ridden team and decided that Casey's best seasons were behind him. Then, year after year, the legend about Casey's fabulous "luck" had grown. Many a reporter who should have known better hid from himself what any fan in the stands could see—that Casey was a baseball master. But now to Casey, as it must come to all winners, came recognition from the press.

"This year Casey's got it in the bag," they said.

Nor was it a matter of having been browbeaten by Casey's amazing string of victories. They based the guess of success for the Yanks in '53 on the amazing players that Casey had to work with. He had Allie Reynolds, Phil Rizzuto, Yogi Berra, Vic Raschi, Ed Lopat, Gene Woodling, Hank Bauer, Gil McDougald, Billy Martin and Johnny Mize. There were promising rookies being brought up by the remarkable Yankee farm system. Casey's player list was filled with young hitting and pitching talent.

And, of course, there was Mickey Mantle, the youngster who had performed so brilliantly in the 1952 World Series. For two years the press had talked about Mantle as a probable successor to the batting laurels won by Joe DiMaggio. Now in 1953 they were already talking about Mantle's great batting feats.

"Mickey ain't even begun to play ball yet," Casey now said. "You ain't seen nothin' yet from that fella compared to what you're gonna be seein' from the lad in years comin' up. This season ought to work out to be his best yet."

And Mickey, never one to willingly let Casey down, tore into the ball like a wild man and crashed out six hits in his first fifteen times at bat. He slugged the ball for a .385 average and was the fire behind every Yankee victory.

His sixteen-game hitting streak right at the start, plus Johnny Sain's masterful hurling, not only sparked the Yanks but sent them right into first place—and kept them there while they piled up a preposterous early-season lead of eleven and a half games over the Cleveland Indians. At that point, all the other teams just about threw in the sponge.

"Mantle ought to be run out of baseball for being unfair competition to all the other teams," growled one non-Yankee fan as he left the Stadium one day after seeing Mickey crash out three straight hits, steal two bases, and then cut off an opposing player's extra-base hit with a brilliant circus catch.

The baseball man of the hour, as that season roared along, was plainly Mickey Mantle. None doubted that 1953 would be his greatest season ever.

The fans, we should note, were impressed by more than mere good playing. Like that day at Griffith Stadium in Washington, for example, when something took place that had never happened in baseball before.

Chuck Stobbs, the Nats' southpaw, had just walked Yogi Berra, with two out in the fifth, when Mantle stepped in to hit. He dug his spikes into the turf and looked up at Stobbs menacingly. His big bat pumped forward once, twice, and then Mickey set himself for the pitch. It was a beauty, fast and right down the outside corner to the right-hand-hitting Yankee star. Mickey took a vicious cut at the ball. *Thwack*—it was a mighty sound as the bat whipped forward driving the ball on a line. On and on the ball rose until it finally was a small speck high in the air. It hung there for a moment and then disappeared over the center-field wall. The huge crowd stared blankly, hardly able to believe that what they were seeing was actually happening. The ball had soared clear over the incredibly high center-field bleachers!

The fans gasped. No one had ever done that before. Not Babe Ruth, baseball's greatest home-run slugger, or Lou Gehrig, or Ty Cobb, or Ted Williams—no one had ever hit a ball that far.

And no wonder! The base of the bleacher wall was 391 feet from the plate. The distance to the back of the wall was 69 feet and the back wall was an additional 50 feet high. For good measure, there was a football scoreboard hanging on top that the ball had to clear. And yet Mickey's drive had cleared the scoreboard and disappeared.

"I've got to get that ball," Arthur "Red" Patterson said. He was a member of the Yank front-office staff and his hobby was collecting balls that had been hit for famous homers.

He raced out of the field and located a youngster who had found and pocketed the ball. His name was Donald Dunaway, and he was ten years old.

"Where did you find the ball, son?" Patterson asked.

"I'll show you," Donald said.

He took Patterson to the back yard of 434 Oakdale Street and pointed to where the ball had landed.

"Is that the exact spot?" asked Patterson.

"Right where I'm showin' you," said Donald.

Patterson bought the ball from the youngster for ten dollars, plus two new balls autographed by Mickey and sent to him later.

Then Patterson went about measuring the hit, and that was how it was discovered that Mickey Mantle had hit the longest home run in the entire history of baseball!

Mickey's blast had traveled the fantastic distance of 565 feet! The distance was verified and all the reporters scrambled to the record books to see whether anyone had ever hit one as far. No player ever had.

It was the most talked-about hit of the season, and veteran baseball stars were now comparing the flashy youngster with Babe Ruth, Lou Gehrig and other long-distance sluggers.

Then the baseball museum at Cooperstown, New York, phoned and asked if they could put the ball on exhibition. "Sure thing," the Yank front office answered. "As soon as we're finished exhibiting it ourselves. We're putting it on display in the Stadium this season, so that all the fans who want to see it can get a chance."

The Big Homer had Casey goggle-eyed.

"I been in this here baseball game for more than forty years now. I've seen hitters in my day. I can tell you that all right. But I never even heard, let alone saw with these old peepers, any right-handed hitter smackin' anything as long as that one. The only right-handed batter from those I saw who I could even begin to compare with Mickey's hit would be Jimmy Foxx. And if you're talkin' about lefties, the only two had power anythin' like this fella was Babe Ruth and Lou Gehrig. So I'll make you a guess: Before Mantle's days are all out, he'll break every long-distance-hitting record in the books. I never seen a young fella with talent and *hitability* like this one."

Then, six days later, Mickey crashed a tremendous drive to the left-center-field fence. It traveled more than 420 feet and everyone agreed that only Lou Gehrig, great Yankee star, and the immortal Babe Ruth had ever hit a ball that far in Yankee Stadium.

So now Mickey's homers were no longer merely counted. It had become the practice to measure them! An amazing tribute to the hitting prowess of the twenty-one-year-old ballplayer!

More important than his long drives, his great clutch hitting when the team needed him also had the fans talking. That second big homer, for example. The Red Sox had tied the score, 2–2, in the ninth inning. Two were out, and the Bombers had two men on when Mickey came up to hit. Could he come through? Would the game go into extra innings? Mickey, batting left-handed against Ellis Kinder, an able right-hander, socked the ball a dozen rows up in the right-field bleachers to bring the Yanks the 6–3 win.

It was a demonstration, at its best, of what it means to a team when a player can come through in the clutch.

The fans were also goggle-eyed about Mickey's speed on the base paths. In spite of his two bad legs, his fleet-footedness had become the talk of the game.

With a stop watch they had actually timed Mickey going down to first base, to see if any man could really be getting there as fast as he seemed to be. And the clockers made the discovery that he was getting there even faster than anyone had imagined! The results, in spite of the fact that the tests were made by a track expert, were so fantastic that even those who held stop watches themselves couldn't believe what the precision timepieces were showing!

From a right-handed start, Mickey raced over the ninety-foot distance to first base in 3.4 seconds after socking the ball and starting to run! Hitting lefty, he zoomed to first in 3.1 seconds!

How right Mutt had been! What a tremendous advantage it was for a righty to be able to switch-hit if he could! Not only could he switch his position at will to confuse opposing pitchers, but he also gained those few precious moments with which to reach first.

But it was his powerful hitting at crucial moments that counted in the team standing and won important games for the Yankees.

In a crucial series with the onrushing Chicago White Sox, pitcher Billy Pierce made one mistake. He gave Mantle a fast ball on the outside corner. Mickey promptly drove the ball 425 feet out of the ball park for the winning runs.

Twenty-four hours later, in St. Louis, they sent in a right-hander to stop Mickey's hitting streak. Mickey switched into a left-handed batting stance. He set himself for the pitch he wanted, then picked out a sizzling fast ball and drove it into the right-center-field stands for a 405-foot homer.

And the more the fans studied the kind of ball he was playing, the more impressed they were. It wasn't just "showy," and it wasn't just great hitting—although anyone would have settled for that. It was a value to the team that could hardly be measured.

The fans thought about the day, for example, when he had smacked a 420-foot homer against the Red Sox. In the same game, he had been on base four times. He had singled in the first and doubled in the sixth. The Sox, to avoid pitching to him, had walked him in the eighth, and he was on when Berra hit his homer. Finally, Mickey put the game on ice with his own homer!

How was the value of such a player to be added up? There was so much more in his playing than even the record was showing. "There's no one in the game this season can compare with Mantle." That was how more and more fans were summing it up.

And the records, even if they didn't show everything, proved clearly that the fans knew what they were talking about. By the middle of June 1953, Mickey Mantle was hitting .347! And he looked as if he was just warming up to his job!

"If the boy's legs only hold out under him," said Casey, "what a season that fella's gonna have!"

And then, as so many times before, the fates again decided to play a trick on Mickey Mantle.

15.

MICKEY lay writhing on the dressing-room table. His face was covered with perspiration. He tried to ignore the pain. He was too busy hoping, praying, that this time he wasn't as badly injured as he had been before. The team needed him; he couldn't be hurt! Not this year, just when everything was going great.

"You'll be up and around in a few days," said the doctor. "You tore up a couple of thigh muscles, but it ought to heal pretty quickly. Got to have plenty of time and lots of rest. Stay off those legs, Mickey," the doctor growled.

In spite of the pain, a grin flickered across Mickey's face. He wouldn't be out for the season. He'd be back playing ball in just a few days!

"Thanks, Doc," he said. "That's the best news I ever heard. I'll get it healed overnight. I got to get back in there."

The doctor's magic worked. In a few days, Mickey was hobbling around.

"How goes it, fella?" asked Casey.

"As good as new. That's how it feels. How about me going in there today?"

Casey smiled. "I like a game ballplayer, I'll tell you that all right. But let's not rush Ma Nature. Let's give her a couple days to do her business. She'll get you healed and back whackin' the ball in no time. Right now all you got to do for yourself is just sit around a little and watch the rest of us try to play ourselves some ball."

Mickey sat on the sidelines and watched. It was torture not to be in there with his teammates. He had been going so good! He had been the spark that lifted the ball club, and he felt awful just sitting around on the bench watching, hoping and praying that he could be in there.

"They say playing ball every day knocks a guy out," he told another player. "I say there's nothing on this earth gets a player exhausted like just sitting around and not being able to get out there and try to help the team."

The Yanks were losing ground. They had begun to slip as soon as Mickey was hurt.

"Heck," said one reporter, "they'd have to slip awful fast to lose this pennant race. When a team has an eleven-and-a-half-game lead, like the Yanks had, they can win by just playing average ball until the season ends."

"But they're not playing average ball. They're playing a lot like minor-leaguers right now."

Then one day Casey put his arm around Mickey's shoulder and said, "All ready to get yourself back in there and win a couple of ball games for us? We sure can use you in there, boy."

"You bet, Casey!"

"Well, get yourself out there to right field, fella, and start playin' ball."

Mickey's face fell. "Right field? I was playing center field when I got hurt."

"The center fielder's got himself a heck of a lot of territory, Mickey. And, believe you me, I ain't anxious to see you runnin' around more'n you need to. Not until you got yourself one-hundred-per-cent okay again."

Mickey was happy once more. He was in there every day, but it wasn't the kind of ball he'd been playing before he hurt his thigh. He just couldn't seem to get started again. In his anxiety to get the team on a winning streak, Mickey was swinging at too many bad pitches. It was the same old habit that had bothered him and almost cost him his job with the Yankees. He was pressing, hitting at bad pitches, popping out and striking out.

"I'll get going in a couple of days," he said.

But he didn't. He was playing raggedly. And as Mickey went, so did the Yankees. They were playing without fire and spirit, dropping game after game.

"Mickey, you ain't really got yourself rested yet," Casey told him. "You look to me like you can use a couple more days just to take it easy sittin' around. So I'd like for you to just take a little more rest."

Mickey was benched!

Mickey Mantle, who had sparked the Yanks in their fantastic winning streak earlier in the season, was benched. Mickey Mantle, who had hit the longest home run in baseball history as the Yanks were racing toward their fifth straight flag, was now sitting it out.

"You think Mantle can come back this season?" fans began to ask each other.

"He'd better," was the usual answer. "Without him, the Yanks look like they're blowing this race for sure. They're just collapsing all over the place."

Mickey didn't stay out long. He was soon back throwing into his playing everything he had, but somehow he wasn't hitting well. He'd get a good wallop, and he'd be sure that the dog days were over. Then he'd watch as the whole team played like a bunch of sandlotters. Neither he nor the rest of the Yanks seemed able to get started again.

"I've never seen any team fall to pieces like the Yanks are doing," fans were saying all over.

The statistics bore out what they said. Mickey had been hurt after the Yanks had run up eighteen straight victories. Then, soon after his injury, they had begun to slump and were soon nose-diving. Their record now showed fifteen defeats in twenty-six starts, including nine consecutive setbacks!

The only thing that kept them in the pennant race at all was their early-season lead of eleven and a half games. And it was being gobbled up fast. Soon after their return from their disastrous third western trip, they were only six games in front of the Cleveland Indians.

From the team that couldn't lose, they had suddenly become the team that couldn't win. That was how baseball men were beginning to see it.

By early August the Yanks had as bad a case of the jitters as they had ever had. They knew that fans were marking them down as the greatest disappointment of the season.

On their victorious second western trip earlier in the season, they had blazed through the hinterlands winning fourteen in a row to stretch their string of wins to eighteen. They had flattened the Indians in three consecutive games.

But now the Cleveland Indians had beaten *them* three times in a row! Worse, the Indians had followed them into the Stadium for a three-game series and had trampled them three more times in a row! Six straight losses to a team they had pushed around mercilessly when they'd been playing championship ball!

The slump showed how important Mantle was to the team. In the past, when he was hitting, the Yanks won. When he didn't hit, they lost. And Mickey, who had been hitting as high as .360 during the Yanks' winning streak, returned from the west batting a trifle over .300. It was a good enough average, no doubt about that. But it wasn't the kind of Mantle hitting that the Yanks needed to pull this season out of the fire.

"Mantle'll start banging them again soon," the die-hard Yank fans said, but other fans thought it was too much to expect of an injured player. Baseball men in general were beginning to say that Casey would need one of his old-time miracles to get his team going again.

"And there's a limit to everybody's share of miracles," they'd add. "Even the Old Professor's."

And then Casey Stengel decided that the time had come for him to take action. So he locked the team in the dressing room and there wasn't a sound from anyone as the Old Professor cleared his throat and got ready to talk.

"Now certain fellas," he roared, "got themselves this here habit of winnin' a pennant in them newspapers. They got themselves the bad luck of bein' able to read the print and they see in this here newspaper, right smack after the season gets goin', that it says them Yank fellas got the pennant right in their pockets for themselves. So what do this type fellas do? They get ready to spend all that World Series money they figure they got in their pocket already. Only nobody tells them they got to win themselves a pennant first!"

One player started to talk but Casey cut him off. "First man talks 'round here finds hisself playin' with Kansas City or some other club in another league."

Smarting from Casey's dressing-down, the club pulled itself together and played as a Yankee team should. In a critical series with the Indians, Joe Collins and Gil McDougald hit successive homers to win in the ninth inning. The next day they handed the Indians another beating and then headed for the big series with the Chicago White Sox.

Virgil Trucks faced the Yanks that blistering hot afternoon at Chicago's Comiskey Park. It was so hot that the fans were sitting in the shade, under the stands. Trucks had the game won going into the eighth inning until he tossed up a fat pitch to Mantle. Mickey promptly drove the ball into the center-field stands for a home run that won the game 3–2. The next day another victory clinched the pennant once more for the happy Bombers.

As the press barged into the dressing room to take part in the victory celebration, Casey put the whole season into a nutshell for them:

"This was a pretty good New York team we got ourselves here. We dropped the ball for a while, but we played good, and that Mantle and Berra and Bauer helped us come out okay like I knew we was gonna do."

For Mickey it had been a disappointing season. Until his injury slowed him down and then forced him out of the game, he had been playing the finest baseball in his career. Then, only after a superhuman effort, a tremendous hitting spurt had lifted his average to near the .300 mark.

But as they celebrated in the dressing room on the afternoon of their new victory, their minds weren't on the record books. They knew that one of the toughest World Series opponents they had ever faced was impatiently waiting to clobber them into dust.

"Save yourselves a little of that pep for the World Series," said Casey, who liked nothing better than to hop from one baseball ruckus into another. "We got to stand up against those Dodgers again."

16.

JUST before the 1953 World Series opened, Rogers Hornsby, the great old-time player, summed up the thinking of thousands of fans.

"If the Dodgers don't beat the Yanks this time, they ought to retire from baseball. They should hang up their baseball spikes for good."

But most fans didn't think it would be necessary for the Brooklyn team to take that drastic step. Despite the tremendous power shown by the Yankees in their winning drive for the pennant, the Dodgers were favored to win. And it wasn't hard to see why.

They had a powerhouse of hitting talent that had battered the life out of the other National League teams. Outfielder Carl Furillo had paced the league's hitters all season. Duke Snider, Jackie Robinson, Gil Hodges, Roy Campanella, were all among the league's top blasters.

But this was only part of the Dodgers' strength. Their morale was tremendous. They played best when the going was hardest. In their furious drive to capture another National League flag, they had won thirty of their last thirty-seven games. They had established a club record of 196 home runs—40 of them by their sensational, hard-hitting catcher Roy Campanella.

But Casey was sure he had the answer to the powerful Dodger bats in his great pitching staff consisting of: Whitey Ford, Eddie Lopat, Vic Raschi, and Johnny Sain. Plus a a man who was a whole pitching staff by himself: Allie Reynolds.

Casey also had Mickey Mantle, who was a menace to the opposing team each time he came up to bat and who was a home-run threat from either side of the plate. Mickey was the big powerhouse of the Yankees, and he had support from Yogi Berra, Hank Bauer, Johnny Mize and Gene Woodling. So the stage was set for a hard fight. And the Dodgers were out for Yankee blood.

Both managers started their ace pitchers. Big Allie Reynolds against Carl Erskine. The Yankees jumped on Erskine from the start; Carl got himself into a peck of trouble in the very first inning by walking Joe Collins, Mantle and Woodling. Then two triples racked up four runs for the Yankees. Allie Reynolds shut out the Brooks until homers by Gil Hodges and George Shuba tied the score, but Johnny Sain put the Dodgers down and the Yankees went on to coast to an easy 9–5 win.

Interestingly enough, it was President Eisenhower who summed up the mood of many fans. He had been visited by Adlai Stevenson, whom he had defeated in the previous year's election, on the day of the first game. When a White House messenger brought in the news that the Yanks had won, the President turned to Stevenson and said, "It's time for a change."

"We got only three more to go," Casey told his team before the second game. "And then it's loafin' all winter. Let's nail ourselves these birds quick."

Mickey Mantle was anxious to get out on the field against the Dodgers for the second game. He had had only one hit in three trips to the plate, but he was happy all over because his close buddy, his best friend, Billy Martin, with three big hits out of four trips to the plate, was the star of the first game. Now he itched to get his big bat going.

But Brooklyn's ace hurler, Preacher Roe, had other ideas. He set the big Yankee sluggers down after a wild first inning in which he walked Woodling, Collins and Mantle. However, just when the Bombers threatened to make a shambles of the game, Roe promptly shut the door in their faces by getting Billy Martin to pop out with the bases loaded.

The game seesawed back and forth until the Yanks tied the score at 2–2 in the seventh inning. The Dodger fans were cheering Roe on, and he pitched masterfully until the eighth frame, allowing the Yanks only three meager hits.

Hank Bauer led off the Yankee half of the inning by rapping a single to left. Roe bore down and forced Yogi Berra to loft a high fly ball to left for out number two.

Then the huge Yankee Stadium crowd of 69,774 fans rent the air with their cheers as Mantle stepped in to hit.

"Give it a ride, Mickey," a fan pleaded.

"C'mon Mantle, out of the park," said another.

Mickey braced himself at the plate and pumped his big bat in a wide menacing circle. He watched Roe's every move.

On the mound, Preacher took his time. He fiddled with his cap, hitched his belt, then toed the rubber for the big pitch. He pumped his arm once, twice, and then fired his best pitch in to Mantle at the plate.

Mickey, poised, waited for the pitch to come within range of his bat. It was a waist-high curve ball, and it broke inside sharply. At the last moment, Mickey drove into the ball with all of his strength. It was a mighty drive. The ball sailed on a line out over Reese's head at short. The ball kept going until it disappeared into the bleachers. The crowd cheered itself hoarse as first Bauer and then Mantle crossed the plate for the winning runs, and the entire Yankee team erupted from the bench and surrounded the happy youngster. They picked him up and carried him off the field in a mad rush of happiness. It was an explosive and exciting finish to a great game.

"How can you beat a team like that?" the fans asked each other as they emptied out of the park. "This Series looks like it's all over."

And then the Dodgers, furious at the jinx that hounded them every time they played the Yanks, fought back furiously. Carl Erskine pitched one of the great games of his career, striking out fourteen Bombers. Mantle was handcuffed all day by Erskine, and he fanned four straight times.

In the eighth inning Roy Campanella drove out a home run to put the game on ice for the Dodgers amid the wildest celebration ever seen in a ball park. Thousands of Dodger fans went berserk with happiness, and they carried Campy off the field as the game ended.

The Dodgers were back in the Series! And they were all the way back the next day when they came out swinging like wild men in the first inning, piled up a three-run lead, and never let up until they had downed New York 7–3.

Two games to two—a brand-new World Series!

"Take it easy," Casey told Mickey before the fifth game started. "Forget about those four strike-outs. Don't let them Dodger fans rattle you. You just keep thinkin' about that homer you wrapped up the second game with. Every day's a brand-new game. We need you cloutin' real good today."

"Right," said Mickey. But the four strike-outs still hurt and he wanted to wipe them off the slate with a vengeance.

In the third inning, a hush settled over the big park. The score was tied 1–1. Hodges made an error, which let in a run, and Podres, who was pitching for the Dodgers, hit Hank Bauer and then walked Yogi Berra. Suddenly the crowd became so silent that the park sounded as if it were deserted. Bases loaded, two out, and Mickey Mantle coming up to bat!

"Why does it have to be Mantle coming up?" a Dodger fan moaned. In spite of his four strike-outs, their respect for his big bat was enormous.

The Dodger fans weren't the only ones who were worried. Chuck Dressen took Podres out and sent Russ Meyer in to stop Mantle.

Mickey looked calm as Meyer got ready. But he couldn't wait for the pitcher to get it across. Here was his chance to shut up those Dodger fans for good about his four strike-outs.

Mickey switched to a right-handed batting stance, waiting for Meyer's southpaw slants. He stood there scowling and confident, his feet wide apart, pumping his big bat forward to ease the tension building up inside him. Meyer toed the rubber and whipped his fast ball in to Mickey.

Crack!

Meyer had whipped it across and Mickey knew, from the solid feel of the bat clouting leather, that he had hit the ball well. It took off and soared high up into the upper stands for a tremendous homer.

Mickey had slammed the very first pitch off Meyer. A grand-slam home run! As four Yank runs scampered home, the huge crowd roared itself hoarse. They filled the air with paper and score cards, and the Yankee bench tore out on the field to carry the deliriously happy Mantle to the clubhouse.

"There ain't many players who can tell you they got themselves a grand-slam homer in a World Series game!" Casey told Mickey, after peeling half a dozen triumphant players off Mickey's back.

Casey was right. Mickey's great drive was only the fourth grand slam in all World Series history. Only three other players had matched what Mickey had just done to Russ Meyer's first pitch. Elmer Smith of the Indians had hit one off the Dodgers 'way back in 1920. Tony Lazzeri of the Yanks had got one off the Giants in 1936, and Mickey's teammate McDougald, as a rookie, had hit one against the Giants at the Polo Grounds.

Mickey's grand-slam homer had knocked the spirit out of the Brooks. The next day the Yanks scored a 4–3 win to end the Series.

Casey Stengel's team had won five straight pennants and five straight world championships! There had never been a team like this in all of baseball history!

As for Mickey, he had triumphed against a succession of injuries that would have sent another player out of baseball. Each time fate struck him down, he got up stronger.

After the previous World Series, Jackie Robinson had publicly said that Mickey Mantle had been the one who had beaten them. In this Series, Mickey's two game-winning homers spoke for themselves.

But perhaps Russ Meyer, who had served up the curve ball that Mickey had knocked into the record books, summed it up best in the remark he made to the press: "When you throw your best pitch and a guy hits it like that Mantle did, there's just nothing you can do about it!"

"And he ain't even got started, he's just a baby yet," Casey said, referring to the many years still coming up for Mickey.

17.

BILLY MARTIN and his pal Mickey Mantle were playing their own version of the pepper game. The game was simple, and they would get a great kick out of their efforts. Before game time each player would throw to the other as hard as he possibly could. Once in a while Mantle would make believe he was the pitcher, and he would try to knock Billy down with a fast ball. Then Martin would scoop up the ball and ram it back just as fast right at Mickey's head. They joked and kidded each other while this took place. It put them in the proper frame of mind for the ball game.

Casey interrupted their activities one day. "Billy, I want to talk with you about something."

Martin came right back at his manager. "So go on talk, Casey. You know this other player. His name's Mantle. You've met him. They call him two-gun Mantle. He shoots 'em dead." He laughed at his outburst, and Mickey joined in the fun.

"This is something private; I got to talk to you all alone."

"Casey, you're kidding. You know I don't have any secrets that Mickey doesn't know about. We're pals.

C'mon, Case. What'd I do now? I haven't had a fight in a long time."

Billy Martin had joined the club late in 1950 and within a year had established his place on the team. A cocky, brash kid from the streets, Martin first played for Stengel when Casey managed the Oakland team of the Pacific Coast league.

Martin was a fine-spirited defensive ballplayer, who turned any ball club into a snarling, fighting pack of players. He was a "take charge guy," and what he lacked in offensive strength, he made up for with his fiery competitive play in the field.

Casey loved the scrappy, street-fighting spirit of Martin. Billy, when he joined the Yankees, took to Mickey immediately, and the two youngsters became inseparable.

"Billy, it's not good news," sighed Casey, "and Mickey ought to be in on this. He'll know in a minute. In a way," sighed the manager, "it's bad news for all of us. But what I got to tell you, Billy, is that George Weiss got a wire—from the U. S. Army. Billy, you're to report for service in three days."

Martin's jaw fell when he realized Casey wasn't joking. "You mean I won't even be able to play a couple of games, Case? How come? I was sure that I could play through the season. The team needs me, and Mickey and I had plans."

"That's out for good. And, son, we're sure gonna miss you out there. You're the guts of the whole team, and I'm gonna miss you. I'll have to do all my fighting with your pal, Mickey."

"Okay, Casey. I'll get ready to go. Gee, I'll miss all you guys." He choked back the tears and looked away.

The news hit Mickey hard. He and Billy were as close as two friends can be. They were roommates during the season and spent practically all their spare time together. They talked over the games and swapped tales, and time passed swiftly when they were together. During the off season Martin had even moved down to Commerce. In Mickey's home town they could be together during the winter to go hunting and fishing.

Now Martin wouldn't be around.

"Gee, Billy, it's a bad break not being able to get through the season."

"You can't blame Uncle Sam. They need a good fighter like me in the Army. How many guys you think we got around like Billy Martin."

Mickey burst out laughing. He always did when Martin started cracking. "Billy, I think they ought to get you a program on TV. You'd have the whole country rockin' with those cracks of yours."

But the laugh didn't last long this time. Martin was going, and that was no joke to Mickey.

"You got no idea how I'd like to go along with you, Billy."

"Who says I got no idea? You told me before how you'd like to get in for a stint. Well, come on in with me. We'd make a great team for Uncle Sam."

"They just won't take me in! Four times already I get called, examined from toe to head, and no dice. 'Osteomyelitis! Go home, Mickey! Maybe you can

143

play ball, but no Army for you. Your leg might go to pieces just like that.'" He snapped his fingers as he spoke.

"I know, Mickey. It's a heck of a bad break. We could have had some real fun there, hey?"

"You bet! Betcha we'd be pretty good soldiers, too."

"The best! Who ever heard about a better team than Mantle and Martin?"

"What gets me," Mickey said, looking by now as sad as Casey, "is some people, they just don't understand. 'Why don't you get yourself into the Army, Mickey?' they write to me. 'Whatcha playin' ball for? Army could use a husky guy like you.' They just don't understand I got turned down four times already!"

"Well, when I get out, we'll have some terrific times again—and some terrific ball games, right?"

"You can say that again!"

But when Martin was all packed and ready to go, Mickey felt as if he were about to lose a brother. "Goodbye, Billy. I'll keep you posted how we're doing."

"Aw, you'll be doing great," said Martin, poking Mickey playfully in the ribs.

Then Martin turned to the assembled reporters. "All I got to tell you boys is the Yanks are still the champs. Nobody wins themselves a pennant until they beat us. We're the best ball club ever." Remembering how much Dodger fans had it in for him, he turned in the direction of Brooklyn, and said, "So long, Brooklyn. Now you're on your own!"

Then the cocky little player walked jauntily off.

"There goes one of the greatest guys you could ever see," said Mickey, and he walked back to the clubhouse.

Martin's departure was blow number two for Mickey that season. The first had come the previous November when he had undergone an operation to remove a floating cartilege from his right knee. The operation had been successful, but the knee was taking its own good time to heal.

"Can I get to play today?" Mickey asked Casey a few days after Martin left.

"Fella," answered Casey, "how many times you got to make me tell you over? No games for you during this here training season! Doc says you'll heal altogether in a month or so. I already lost myself Martin. I want you should rest that leg. If I see you swattin' even one ball, I'll get myself a stick and give you some swattin' myself."

"Aw, all right."

"And I got to know," Casey added, "you're keepin' that there iron lead in your shoe to get that leg strong. Mainly, you got orders you ain't to be doin' nothin' till I tell you. Now, you understand that, Mr. Mantle. I got to have you in tiptop shape when we start to move. Okay?"

Casey's precautions were sound. Mickey was far from ready to play yet. The knee could act up at any minute, and his right thigh muscles and tendons were very weak. His legs would need all the rest they could get in order to stand up under the battering of a big-league season.

In spite of his injuries, the reporters were predicting a banner season for Mickey. Some said this would be his best year.

"You want to know what I'll bet this year?" he said to the reporters. "Well, I don't look at it that way. This year I'll be glad if I can play out a whole season. So long as I'm in there every day, I'll figure I'm doin' okay."

As it turned out, Mickey was being more realistic that year than the press.

Halfway through May, the baseball world knew the Yanks were in trouble. Worse, the Yanks knew it, too, even though they tried to spark themselves into playing better ball. The big hitters slumped. The pitching of Reynolds, Raschi and Lopat, the big three of Casey's staff, was falling apart.

"Casey," the reporters asked, "when will Mantle get back into shape?"

"I got the announcement from the doc. He says he expects a month from now Mantle'll be all healed up. It ain't his fault he ain't been catchin' fire. We played him too quick. We shoulda let him rest a lot more."

The familiar Mantle power was there, but he lacked consistency. He didn't get those big hits when they were needed. But when he cut loose, fans howled as joyfully as ever.

Batting against Morris Martin of the Athletics, for example, Mickey had walked slowly to the plate and waited. The fans expected nothing. He hadn't been hitting. And then—*whosh!*—he unleashed a 425-foot homer. Just the kind of blow that had "Mantle" written all over it. A tremendous whack. And then his bat became silent again and the team slumped with him.

But Mantle was only one problem. Casey had almost a whole teamful that season. The Yanks just weren't coming through as often as necessary. There was a sluggish air about the five-time champs. They were doing their best, but that certain magic that had become the Yank trademark was gone.

In June, Mantle started to hit again. In a game against the Red Sox, he blasted out a homer, a double and a single. He followed that up by hitting in ten straight games and drove his average up to .307 with nine homers.

He tried vainly to push his average higher, but he just couldn't seem to regain his magic touch. And the more he pressed and fought to keep the pennant race alive, the more he slipped.

Casey was pouring advice and hoping to get a fire going, but he also was worried. Casey knew the trouble, and he knew that the glories of past seasons wouldn't get him a pennant this time unless the club suddenly caught fire.

Instead of catching fire, they slipped badly. The heartbreaker came in Chicago against the Sox. The Yanks, trying desperately to get back into the race, lost one that put them six and a half games behind. The date was September 22, and by then even a few miracles wouldn't have been enough.

General Manager Frank Lane of the White Sox

couldn't restrain his joy. "Oh, Casey," he yelled in Comiskey Park after the game, "let's see how good you are now!"

Casey, however, was realistic. "We had ourselves a chance until we dropped those three games in Boston," he said. In that one series, the Red Sox had socked the Yanks—who had been only two and a half games behind when the series started—to five and a half games behind the Indians.

The Yanks had reacted to the three-game loss with fury, and had come back to win six games in a row. But that was all they had left. The team came apart at the seams. They dropped eight of their next sixteen, and that was that.

At season's end the Indians were eight games ahead. And it was as good as eighty. For the first time in six years, Casey's team wouldn't be in the World Series.

But in baseball history, 1954 will forevermore be famous for a very unusual reason: It was "the year the Yankees *lost* the pennant and Mickey Mantle, the superstar of the Yankees, failed to rise to the heights expected of him." He was the new super-great, hailed by experts as "As good as DiMaggio, and every bit as good a slugger as Babe Ruth and Lou Gehrig." Mickey proved to be one of the biggest disappointments of the year.

"Wait till next year," said Mickey, as he hurriedly packed his bag and headed west to Commerce.

18.

THE sun flooded Miller Huggins Field in St. Petersburg, Florida. The weather was the kind that made a man feel good just to be alive. The Yankees were limbering up, getting the winter kinks out of their legs. They were romping around, tossing the ball, playing pepper games. It was baseball time once more and every player on the field was glad to be there.

Casey sat on the bench and took in the scene. He felt pretty good and told himself that he had no special worry about the coming season. And yet, a particular worry kept bothering him. It had been bothering him, on and off, all winter.

Casey was more than a little worried about Mickey Mantle. He felt he ought to have a serious talk with the young player but he didn't want to antagonize him. Casey hoped that he might not have to have the conference with Mantle.

It looked as if he wouldn't have to when the season opened. Mickey began 1955 play with a bang. In the first game, against Washington, he blasted three hits, one of them a tremendous homer. But then he stopped hitting. At the end of an eighteen-game stretch his batting average nosed down to .258.

The time had come for the talk Casey had planned.

"Mickey," he said, "you got me goin' round talkin' to myself. I just don't know how to figure you out."

Mickey didn't say a thing. He knew he hadn't been hitting, and he couldn't figure why.

"It's not just you ain't hittin'," Casey told him. "It's *why* that's got me good and riled up."

Mickey still didn't say anything. Casey's face showed how worked up he was.

"Mickey, I got this on my mind a long time to tell ya. I worked with you and talked to you, had the coaches work with you till I'm blue in the face, but then you go out and play your own game like you didn't hear a word from me. Now I guess you know I think you got it in ya to be like Ruth and DiMaggio. But you ain't doin' it! You're not even comin' close! All that natural ability goin' to waste, that makes me mad."

"Casey, I'm out there always trying my best. I'm just not hitting right."

"You ain't tryin' nothin'. You're not even listenin'. Take last year. If Mantle was just an everyday-type player on a team, I'd say he played okay for hisself. But for Mantle you played miserable. You got yourself more natural speed and power than anyone I ever seen, and what're you doin' with it? Not a thing!"

"Casey, I'm out there fighting for base hits all the time."

"You're not fighting for hits. You want to send every

ball over the fence. I tell you to meet the ball, time it, bunt the pitch once in a while, just to keep the other team off balance. You're not even listening. Last year, fella, you fanned a hundred and seven times for yourself! Fella don't fan a hundred and seven times 'less he's tryin' to knock the leather offa the ball every time! Why, you can raise your average fifteen, twenty points just by shortening your swing and getting on base with a bunt once in a while. But what are you lookin' for? Hits or yells from the stands over the long-distance homers?"

"Casey, I—"

"You ain't heard me out," Casey said firmly. "A fella can't listen and talk at the same time. The thing gripes me most is I don't know if you care for this game at all. I see you doin' things your way, takin' it easy. Maybe I say to myself everything came too easy for him. Up from those minors overnight. Why, I had to fight like a looney for everything I got for myself. I was a young ballplayer didn't have your natural speed and power. But I used what I got. I watched them pitchers eagle-eyed. I ran out everything for myself, even little scratch infield hits. I threw my whole strength into the game. Maybe you just don't care. If a ballplayer don't care, it don't matter how much he's a natural!"

"Casey, you got me all wrong. You got to remember sometimes it takes a player a little time to really get to know the ropes. I'm out there tryin' to learn all the time. And this year I feel great. I really feel I'm gonna do very good for myself this season once I get started."

"The leg feels good, huh?" Casey asked.

"Feels like new."

"Mickey," Casey said in a softer tone. "I don't want you should get the wrong idea. I ain't tryin' to turn you into no singles hitter. I know Ruth and all those big hitters fanned a lot of times, but I want you to be the greatest of them all. I want you to work. Work on your weak points. Think about the game twenty-four hours a day. That's what Ty Cobb did, and Hornsby and Williams and Stan Musial. And that's what I want you to do. So far, Mickey, in the years that you been with us, you won a lot of games for us and I'm not for-gettin' it, but you got to take this business more serious. You got to *care,* to be the best player in the game."

"Nobody cares more than me, Casey. Ever since I was a baby, all I know is baseball. It's my whole life, and I just feel that this is gonna be my big year. I just got that feeling, Casey."

"Then show me how much you care when you get out on that field. That's the place it counts. Not just in talkin'."

"You'll see, Casey."

"You bet I'll see. I'll be on that bench *lookin'* all the time."

And then Mickey set out to prove to the Old Pro-fessor that he wasn't just talking. His bat began doing the talking for him.

It was a pleasant spring day. In the morning the sky had been overcast but now as the sun broke through, the crowd cheered. The fans were bent forward in their seats waiting for the game to get under way.

"I hear Casey's pitchin' Tom Morgan today," said one fan. "Good reliable pitcher, that Morgan."

"It's Steve Gromek for the Tigers. It's been announced. But I hope to heck it's not gonna be a pitcher's duel. I come up to the Stadium to see myself some hittin'. Number Seven out there's my man. That Mickey Mantle! I can't tell ya what a kick I get outa that boy slammin' one!"

"Well, we'll soon see what your guy can do for hisself against Gromek," answered the first bleacherite.

The two fans, and the crowd, didn't have to wait. The action started in the first inning.

Morgan set the Tigers down in order in the first inning, fanning three men in succession. Then third baseman Andy Carey noticed that outfielder Jay Porter was playing first base for the Tigers. So Carey said to Casey: "Say, Case. Look, Porter's playin' first. I think I could drag-bunt down the first-base line. That could be a tough one even for a seasoned first sacker. But he's an outfielder and maybe he won't know how to handle it. What d'ya say?"

"Try it," Casey answered. "This here game's young. But when you bunt it, try to drop it halfway up the line, so the pitcher and that fella on first both got to go for it. Then run your head off!"

"I'm runnin' already," said Carey, walking to the batter's box.

The play worked out just as he had hoped it would.

153

Gromek and Porter both scrambled for the bunt and Carey was safe on first before the Tigers could get themselves organized.

The next batter was Mantle.

Gromek was a right-hander, so Mantle shifted into a left-handed batting position. Then he stood calmly at the plate, pumping his bat forward, waiting for the pitch he wanted.

"Gromek, I got pity on you!" Carey taunted from first. "Mantle's gonna lose your ball on you!"

Gromek sailed one letter high across Mickey's chest and Mickey let the ball go by. Gromek zipped a fast one across now, and once again Mantle's bat didn't move. Mickey glanced at Casey, got a nod and tightened his grip on the bat. The next ball was a fast curve and Mickey caught it as the ball zipped across the plate. He timed the curve beautifully and drove the ball into the center-field stands for a two-run homer.

In the third inning Bauer bunted and beat the throw to the bag. He raced to second as Andy Carey's ground ball was smothered for the out.

The crowd screamed in excitement as Mantle stepped in to hit. Mickey was all business as he flexed his shoulders, pumped his big bat forward and waited for Gromek's first offering. It came in fast and on the outside, and the umpire shouted, "Ball one."

"Let's see another homer now!" a fan shouted. "C'mon, Mickey," a thousand voices roared, "hit the ball."

Mickey stepped back out of the box, dipped his

hands into the dirt, wiped them off on his pants, then stepped in once more.

Gromek hunched over, pumped his arm around and whipped in another fast ball. Mickey promptly drove the pitch into center field for a single, scoring Hank Bauer.

So it was 3–0 now and Mantle had driven in all three runs with his homer and single. But he wasn't through for the day.

Next time up, he took Gromek's first pitch and socked it 430 feet into the right-center section of the bleachers. The bases were empty and Mickey came racing home for the fourth Yankee run, as the entire crowd of 50,000 fans roared their approval.

Casey was beaming with a that's-my-boy smile. "Maybe, Mick, I should send the rest of the fellas to a movie for the day. You ain't givin' them nothin' to do. You're hittin' this Gromek fella like he's off the sand-lots, and all the runs we got is yours."

"I like the way Gromek pitches," Mickey said, grinning.

"The funny thing," Casey said, looking thoughtful, "he's not pitchin' such bad ball. Nobody's gettin' much offa him, only you. But he's already four runs in a hole. They'll take him out for sure."

"I hope not," said Mickey.

But Casey was right. When Mickey came up in the eighth, Gromek was no longer pitching. On the mound for the Tigers was southpaw Bob Miller, a new addition to the team. The Tigers hoped somebody

155

could stop Mantle's big bat. Maybe young Miller could do it.

Mickey's answer was to switch into a right-handed hitting position against the southpaw. And then, with the crowd barely settled back to watch the duel between Mantle and Miller, Mickey slammed the first pitch into the top of the stands for his third home run of the day.

The crowd gasped and then jumped to its feet. The cheer was one of the loudest that had ever been heard in the Stadium.

The Yankee players stared at Mickey with a kind of awe. They'd seen Mantle have tremendous days before, but this one was for the record books. Three homers and a single in four times at bat! Homers from each side of the plate—right-hand and left-hand—*in the same game!*

This was the kind of ball playing that Casey knew Mickey had in him, and that he wanted to see. Naturally, he didn't expect such exhibitions every day. It was the kind of feat that makes a player remembered if he can bring it off even once in a whole career. But Casey knew Mickey had many such days in him. He knew that Mickey had seasons of greatness in him if he just bore down.

But the thing that made him happiest was the way Mickey was listening to him. He was out there in earnest. He was no longer indifferent and he played every ball as if a pennant hung in the balance.

As the season raced into May, the important story was that Mickey was just now developing a consistency that he had never shown before. Two days later Mickey slammed out a bases-loaded homer off pitcher Mike Fornieles to beat Chicago in the eighth frame.

On May 16 he was batting a solid .311. He'd just finished a remarkable weekend. He'd hit four for four against the Tigers, two for four against them the next day, and four for nine at Yankee Stadium in a double-header with Kansas City.

His hitting streak was the talk of the league. The rest of the team rallied behind him and played first-rate ball.

By June 1 Mickey had put together one of base-ball's great hitting records. During a five-game span, Mantle got on base safely fifteen times in a row. He belted a homer, a triple, two doubles, a single, was walked nine times and reached first once on an error. It was a fantastic hitting spree.

On the night of June 21 Mickey strode to the plate at the Stadium against pitcher Alex Kellner of the Kansas City Athletics. He drove Alex's first pitch on a towering line 'way out to the far reaches of the wall at the 461-foot mark in center field.

Bob Wilson, the A's center fielder, started after it with the crack of the bat, turned once, put on the steam and then stopped dead in his tracks. He stared completely amazed as he saw the ball shoot over the outfield fence at the 461-foot mark and take another 25 feet to land.

In the hullabaloo that followed, veteran Yank fans agreed it was one of the longest homers ever hit in the Stadium. Bill Dickey, whose memories of Yankee

157

Stadium ball went back a long way, said, "I remember one Lou Gehrig hit off of Willie Sherdel back in the '28 World Series. It went on a line to where Mantle's hit went, but it smacked into the screen and didn't have the carry Mickey's homer had."

Then he added this: "I'd say this was the longest home run I'd ever seen hit into the center-field bleachers. What makes it all the more terrific is that the ball Mickey hit was a change-up. Mickey had to supply all the power."

Then suddenly, it was time off for the All-Star game in Milwaukee. Mickey was in for the Yanks and the American League, and he wanted to make a good showing.

"Hey, Mick," said one of the other American League players, "you belt our pitchers around plenty for homers. So how about doing something today for *us?* Think you can sink one in the stands?"

"I'll try. You bet."

Mickey looked around the jammed park and listened to the 45,000 fans roar for action. He looked over the lineup and knew he was surrounded by the baseball stars of both leagues. He was anxious to play and was impatient for the game to start.

"Listen to those fans," Mickey said to another American League player.

"There ain't no mistakin' where they stand. The N.L. got this crowd in their pocket. They're waitin' up there for them Nationals to clobber us."

"Well," said Mickey, "the way to get them cheerin' for us is by our hittin'."

In the third inning the game suddenly came alive. Robin Roberts, pitching for the Nationals, let Kuenn reach him for a single, and Fox sent one into short right-center, advancing the men to third. Roberts then blew sky high—he wild-pitched a run across and walked the next hitter.

There were two on when Mickey stepped to the plate.

A huge roar went up from the pro-National crowd. There were plenty of jeers too, but the majority of the crowd wanted to see Mickey hit the ball, and he wanted to oblige them.

He waited tense and anxious. Roberts was fast and had a good head. Boy, he could fool you. Mickey wanted to hit a long one so badly it hurt him. He nervously shifted his feet, dug in at the plate and waited for the pitch.

Roberts toed the rubber, glanced around at the base runners, kicked his left leg high and then flashed a fast ball in. It fairly sizzled as it roared toward the plate and Mickey, swinging at just the right moment, smashed it over the center-field screen for a three-run homer. The din of the excitement and roar of the crowd was thunderous, and the game was held up for fully five minutes as excited spectators leaped over the railings to shake Mickey's hand and to pummel his back. But the Nationals won the game, one of the most grueling all-star games on record, as Stan Musial blasted a twelfth-inning homer for a 6–5 victory for his side.

Next day the headline read: NL STARS BEAT AL

IN MILWAUKEE. But right below it was another: MANTLE CLOUTS THREE-RUN HOMER.

Mickey's team had lost. But every fan agreed that he had done more than his share. He had played great ball.

By the end of August the pennant race had turned into a rat race. The Yankees, White Sox and Indians were neck and neck around first place and it was anybody's race. The Yanks, though, had sagged badly and then, in a complete reversal of form, had dashed off a winning streak taking ten out of eleven games.

"Like I told ya right at the start," Casey said, "every little game is it. Right now any one of them little games could mean we win or lose. We're not givin' anything away. We're goin' right through this league and play every game as if it's the last one, and we're gonna win. Right?"

"Right!" the players roared back. There was fire in all of them. They knew they *had* to take this pennant. If they lost, they might lose a lot more in the seasons ahead. This was a turning point for the Yanks. Would they remain losers? Or would they once again become the fabulous, winning Yanks?

On September 4, Cleveland was in first place, by half a game. The Yanks were matched against the Senators and they knew they couldn't afford to lose that day's game. It could mean the end of their pennant chances.

Bob Turley was on the mound for the Yankees. He walked Eddie Yost and Ernie Oravetz, the first two men he faced. Casey was so keyed up, and so sure that the umpire had mistaken a strike for a ball, that he ran out of the dugout and blew steam at Red Flaherty, the umpire, who promptly sent him to the showers.

It was a furious Casey who stormed off the field. His men were in this crucial game, and he wouldn't even be there to help them!

"Win, win, win!" he yelled at his players as he walked off the field.

So it was up to the Yanks now to save the day, and maybe the pennant, on their own. Bob Turley bore down and finished the inning with two Senators on base. At least that crisis was past.

Now the Yanks came to bat with the do-or-die spirit that Casey had pounded into them. Facing them was Pedro Ramos, who quickly got himself into trouble by letting two Yanks on, with Mickey Mantle coming up next.

Could Mantle come through? He'd already blasted thirty-six homers in this '55 season to keep the Yanks in the race for first place. Could Mantle hit one now?

His answer was a tremendous blast that sent three runs in. It was homer number thirty-seven of the season. More important, it knocked the starch out of the Senators in that first inning. It gave Casey the big victory that he had wanted—and he got it just a few minutes after he was booted off the field.

Then something happened that made Mickey happier than anything else that could have happened. He was in the locker room putting on his uniform before the next game, when his buddy Billy Martin walked in.

Billy, looking jauntier than ever in his army uniform, grinned and said, "Hey, Mickey. Look who's here for a visit!"

"Billy, you look great! Better even than when you left!"

"The army's pretty good to a man. They feed him good, make him get a lot of rest. And I've been playing a lot of ball, like I've been writing you. Managing and playing for the Fort Carson team's been a lot of fun."

"Billy, it's like old times seeing you here. I hope you can stay for the game."

"Heck, I came for some real fun. I think I'll go out there and bat a few around. Maybe I can bring in a run or two for my old Yank pals."

Then Martin started peeling off his Army shirt.

"Billy, can you do that?" Mickey asked, looking worried. "The Army got rules you know. It'd be great to see you in a game again, but I don't want you to get in trouble, maybe court-martialed."

"Relax!" Martin answered. "I'm out. I gotta go back to Carson at the end of the month for final discharge papers, but I'm out now."

Mickey threw his arms around Martin, "Billy, you're back for good!"

"Sure am. Now where's that old suit of mine?"

Said Stengel happily to the press, "Martin should help us, whether at short, or at second, or even just sitting on the bench. He will help the spirit of this club."

Sparked by Mickey's hitting and by Martin's return, the Yanks went on a winning rampage in the home stretch. They drove themselves into first place and held it.

The Yanks were pennant winners again! Casey's "fellas" had brought home the bacon. It was like old times again. The one losing season was behind them. "Yanks" and "winners" once again were words the fans said in one breath.

"Now that's what I say is a heck of a lot more like it!" Casey told his beaming team. "Who in heck ever heard such a thing as Yanks bein' losers? It's our pennant. Belongs to us. Now we got it back!"

19.

THE Dodgers knew that when they took the field against the Yankees in this World Series there would be a tenth man on their team whose name wasn't on their player list—Mr. Jinx. Obviously he was the cause of their unending Series defeats. There was no other explanation.

Seven times in modern baseball history the Brooklyn team had gone through their Series paces with complete confidence, only to go down to defeat seven times. No matter how great the Dodgers were during the season, they fell apart during the Series. No matter how battered their opponents had been from their season's labors, they gained strength during the tussle with the Dodgers.

And of all their opponents, none had the Dodgers more bothered and bewildered than the Yankees.

Would this year be different? Would Walt Alston's tough Dodger team finally break the hex that was driving them to despair?

Yankee fans were confident. Only one thing bothered them. It looked as if Mantle would view this World Series from the bench.

"Right now," Mickey told the press, "I can hardly

stand, but I want to get in there and play. The worst thing in baseball is to sit on the bench. Especially in a World Series. You play your head off all year for the big Series, and then to think of sitting on the bench kills me. But it's up to Casey. If he says sit, I'll sit."

"You take it easy, fella. Stop givin' yourself a hard time. Think about that there leg a little. I'll use you maybe if we need a long belt in a pinch. Just you sittin' on the bench is like poison to those Dodgers. I'll just sit you there, lookin' healthy and strong, and let those fellas see you. Even the sight of you on the bench is enough to scare those Dodgers."

Mickey sat down glumly. "Just keep me in mind, Casey. Don't forget all about me. I want to get in there if I can."

"If I can get you in there for a turn or two, okay. But I ain't playin' ya in the Series, and I ain't arguin' about it."

Mickey watched the entire first game from the bench, and he cheered himself hoarse as the Yankees' part-time first baseman, Joe Collins, pounded out two tremendous homers to knock off the Dodgers 6–5.

Next day Dodger gloom deepened. Tommy Byrne, a southpaw who had been sent down from the majors and then brought up again, gave the Brooks only five measly hits for the day. The Yankees weren't hitting, but that didn't bother Byrne. He contributed a smashing base hit that netted the Bombers four big runs, while he held the Dodgers to two runs for another big Yankee win.

Two games played, two victories for the Yanks!

The Yanks yelled it up after the second game. "Only two more games to go," cried Hank Bauer in the dressing room. "It's in the bag. We're in."

Mickey Mantle sat quietly in front of his locker as he watched Berra and Bauer horse around. Finally he walked over to Casey.

"I feel okay, I just can't sit on the bench any more. I got to play tomorrow. What do you say, Case?"

"I been watchin' you walkin' around. I'll let you play if you watch out for that leg. You can't take any chances," Casey said.

"I'll be careful," Mickey said quickly as Casey nodded approval.

Mickey went in, but it was the Dodgers' day. Despite the fact that the leg pained him terribly throughout the game, Mickey connected for a home run off Johnny Podres. Podres pitched airtight ball while his mates aided by a Roy Campanella homer piled up an 8–3 win.

"Mantle's the same as ever," sports editor Max Kase reported. "Mickey Mantle played his heart out yesterday in one of the gamest exhibitions we've ever seen. He played with a bad shoulder, a bandaged knee and still looked like the best player on the field."

Ignoring the pain, Mickey somehow played through the entire fourth game. But he just wasn't his real self. He had to be content with one lonely base hit. The Yanks as a team couldn't keep pace with the powerful Brooklyn slugging. The Dodgers, playing as if their lives depended on a win, routed five Yank pitchers. They slammed out fourteen hits, and three were homers by Campanella, Hodges and Snider. Final score: Dodgers 8, Yanks 5.

Brand-new Series! Tied! Two games to two!

"Let's get ourselves goin'," Casey told a Yank team that was now a little bewildered.

"Just two more takes it for us!" Alston yelled at the Dodgers, who had been counted out of the running just two games before. "There ain't no jinx round here. There are only pitchers out there waiting for you to slam their pitches for hits!"

Mantle watched the action of the fifth game from the bench. His entire body was racked with pain; he felt helpless and miserable as he watched Duke Snider drive out two home runs. Bob Cerv and Yogi Berra put the Yanks back into the ball game with home runs, but another long blast by Sandy Amoros, and the Dodgers had the all-important fifth game all wrapped up 5–2.

Walt Alston was beaming. "Just one more does it!" he told his jubilant team. "C'mon now boys, we got those Yanks on the run."

It was a tense Yankee team that got ready to play the sixth game. They couldn't afford to do anything wrong. Lose this one, and there'd be no others to play.

"You can do it!" Mickey told his teammates as they waited in the dugout for the game to start. "C'mon now, let's get on those Dodgers and take their hides." Then he smacked the bench angrily. "I'd give anything to be gettin' into this one."

The Dodger crowd was yelling, "Play Ball!" They couldn't wait for the Dodgers to wrap it up.

Rizzuto walked to open the game and then brought the crowd to its feet by stealing second. Yogi Berra picked out a good pitch and lined it to center as Rizzuto scored. Before the inning was over the Bombers had crashed out five runs to put the game on ice. The Dodgers were throttled throughout the game and the final score was 5–1.

Three games to three! The last game would decide the Series!

On the evening before the seventh game, the fans had some strange discussions, pre-game talk about the players on the different teams and about the probable pitchers. But now the fans were talking about whether the Dodgers could break their jinx, and whether the Yanks could remain unbeatable in World Series play. The fans sounded like voodoo experts.

And then, after a game that was a heartbreaker for the Yanks, the Series was over! The Dodgers had finally won! The "jinx" was no more! Despite eight hits off Podres, the Yanks had been unable to convert any of them into a run. The Dodgers, meanwhile, picked up two runs and that was enough to wrap up the biggest victory in modern times for the Brooklyn Dodgers, for it gave them a World Series triumph over their bitter rivals from the Bronx.

The Dodger fans went wild. Miracle of miracles, the Dodgers had finally won a World Series!

"Let 'em enjoy it," Casey said glumly. "We're gonna get it back from them next year. Just wait and see."

Alone and dejected, Mickey Mantle sat on a stool in

front of his locker. He was hunched over and his hands covered his face. It's all my fault, he thought to himself. If I had been in shape to play we would have won. We should have beaten those Dodgers. One day it's my shoulder, the next day my ankle, then it's my knee. I just can't seem to play without hurting. Maybe it would be better if Casey would use someone else in my place. They could do better than a gimpy, one-legged ballplayer.

He glumly brushed aside the sympathetic gestures of his teammates, and then Casey walked over and put his arm around Mantle.

"Son, I want you to be a tough loser. That shows that you want to win, but don't go blamin' yourself for losin' the Series. Just you remember this here Yankee club is a team. The whole team got beat and just so you won't forget that, I want to tell you here and now that one of these here seasons you're gonna bust out and be the big man of this here team, and I wouldn't be surprised if it happens next year. Now come on, son, pack your bags, you and me is gonna do a little fishin' and relaxin'. Next year we'll get those Bums."

Mickey stood up, wiped his face clean, broke into a slow grin and then impulsively threw his arms around Casey. He hugged him in a quick burst of gratitude and said, "Casey, you're the greatest."

20.

NOT since the days of Babe Ruth had the entire baseball world fixed its attention on one man as it did in 1956. And that man was Mickey Mantle!

"Is this the year in which Mickey Mantle ties or breaks Ruth's 1927 record of sixty home runs?"

The clamor for Mickey to break Ruth's record started during spring training and it was stepped up so powerfully as the season went along that the 1956 pennant race itself took a back seat. In fact, Mantle's slugging brought the Yanks the pennant so early that the other teams just about threw in the towel and waited—like everybody else—to see if Mantle could outhit the fabled Babe.

Once the spring training games started, Mickey blasted off to a flying start. He smashed homers over the fence at Miller Huggins Field. In Miami he drove a ball over a center-field fence for the first time in the history of that ball park. He blasted homers at St. Petersburg. On the exhibition tour he hit a homer in Cincinnati that had the fans and sportswriters amazed. He had a new air of confidence and authority.

Billy Martin squatted alongside his teammate

Hank Bauer. Bauer nodded his head slowly. "Yeah! I see what you mean. There is something strange—I mean different—about Mickey. He talks differently, acts differently. Look at the way he's standing up there at the plate. Even that's different."

"That's only part of the story, Hank. I can't put my finger on it, but I'll tell you he's not the same Mantle. Why he used to horse around and fool around with me before practice games. We played a game and tried to knock each other down with tricky pitches. But now we don't play any more. I get a snappy Hello, and off to the batting cage for Mantle."

"Yeah! I see that," said Bauer, "and I also know that he's been spending a lot of time talking with Bill Dickey and Frank Crosetti. He's asking them a lot of questions about his batting stance and—"

"Look at him now. He's in that cage again," said Billy.

Across the field, Mickey stepped briskly into the batting cage and squared away to face pitcher Johnny Kucks.

"All right, young fella, let 'er go."

Kucks looked across at Mickey and fired his fast ball in to the plate. It was a tight pitch, high up on the hands. Mickey stepped in, whipped his bat viciously at the ball and sent it soaring high and far into the center-field stands, more than four hundred feet away.

Kucks followed the flight of the ball, then turned back to Mantle. "Nice belt, Mickey. A homer in any park."

"Okay, let's try it again," said Mickey. "I want the

same pitch, tight, right up on the hands. I couldn't hit them last year. Keep on throwing, Johnny."

Kucks nodded his head, stepped into the rubber and came down with the identical pitch. This time Mickey powdered the ball into the left-field seats. Once more Kucks fired the ball in to Mantle, and once again Mickey hammered it out.

It was a tremendous display of hitting power and every player on the field that day stopped to watch Mantle in action. When Mickey had had enough he left the cage and trotted over to the dugout. He grinned as Martin and Bauer looked up at him.

"I got to work some more on those tight close pitches tomorrow. Nobody is gonna fool me with those sucker pitches this year. Now I'm gonna do my ten laps around the field. Got to get my legs in great shape this year. Can't afford any time off for injuries. See you at dinner." He was off and running before Billy or Hank could answer him.

"I think," said Bauer, "that our country cousin from Commerce is gonna be quite a ballplayer this year. He's older, more experienced, and now for the first time in five years he's serious about filling Joe DiMaggio's shoes. That's the way I size him up this year, Billy."

"You know, Hank"—Martin turned to watch Mantle run his ten laps out—"a lot of pitchers are gonna be surprised this year. Mickey's not gonna be easy to fool. Have you noticed he's standin' further back in the batter's box, and he's beltin' those tight pitches on his hands. Last year he fanned on those pitches.

And another thing, Hank," Billy said, "he's older, more sure of himself, and he's confident that he can slug any pitcher in the game."

"And he's smarter, too," said Bauer. "I'm glad I don't have to play against him."

"You can say that for me too, Hank," Martin agreed solemnly. "I think this is the year Mantle will be Mister Big."

Mickey had never worked harder than he did for the 1956 season. He was like a thoroughbred waiting at the starting gate. When the spring training games started, early in March, Mickey started his hitting barrage. In Miami against the Dodgers he drove two successive pitches over the center-field fence for two long home runs. The next day back at St. Petersburg Mickey lost a ball in deep center field for another homer. On the trip homeward, Mantle blasted long drives in Jacksonville, Savannah and Atlanta.

Reporters and fans recalled that Mickey had slammed thirty-seven homers in 1955 and had won the American League's homer crown. He had done it in spite of having been out for part of the season and in such poor condition that he was able to play in only two World Series games.

President Ike Eisenhower opened the 1956 season for the Washington Senators by tossing out the first ball, and Mantle promptly grabbed the spotlight by driving pitcher Pascual's first pitch on a line over the center-field fence for one of the longest home runs ever seen in Washington. In the sixth inning with two Yankees on base Mickey again slashed a long drive over the center-field fence. It was the first time that any player ever hit two homers over the center-field barrier in a single game in the spacious Washington ball park. The huge crowd of 27,837 spectators, led by President Eisenhower, joined in a tremendous roar of applause for the young slugger. After the game, Mickey was escorted to the President's private box. As the young man approached him, the President thrust his hand out and shook Mickey's hand. "Mickey, that was powerful slugging you did this afternoon. I don't think I've ever seen anyone ever hit a ball farther."

Mickey was awed and embarrassed. "Thank you very much, Mr. President. Thank you very much." That was all he could say, and as soon as the President sat down Mickey sprinted to the Yankee dugout.

It was a day he would never forget. Here he was, Mutt Mantle's son, from Commerce, Oklahoma. Six years ago he had been just a kid in high school. Then he worked alongside his father down in the shafts of the Blue Goose mines. Now this was 1956, and today the President of the United States had shaken his hand in public before thousands of fans. How he wished that Mutt were here today!

Three days later the Yankees opened their home season against their old rivals, the Boston Red Sox. The players lined up to receive their 1955 pennant rings, the band played, and New York's Mayor Robert F. Wagner and manager Casey Stengel hauled up the big Yankee pennant-winner's flag to the top of Yankee Stadium.

The Yankee's pitching ace Whitey Ford held the slugging Bo-Sox to just five hits, while his mates, led by Mickey Mantle, blasted out a 7–1 victory. Mantle drove in four runs with a towering homer and a bunt single. However, Mickey injured his ankle in beating out the bunt and had to leave the game in the seventh inning.

Five days later, against Kansas City, Mantle staged a one-man batting show, slugging two long homers and then outsmarting the Athletics' infield by beating out a bunt in the seventh inning to spark the Bombers to a 5–2 win. It was Mickey's ninth home run, and it boosted his batting average to a stunning .443. Two days later Mickey teed off in the seventh inning of a game against the Cleveland Indians to drive out another four-bagger and snatch certain victory from the Cleveland club.

Now, for the first time in his career, Mickey was living up to all of his expectations. Singlehandedly he sparked the Yankee ball club to victory after victory. In game after game he drove out smashing home runs to pile up decisive wins for the team. Catcher Yogi Berra shared some of the heavy hitting duties with Mickey, and the two men were the scourge of every pitcher in the league.

When the fans began to compare Mickey's great hitting with that of Babe Ruth, he brushed it all away. "Fellas, believe me," he told the sportswriters, "I'm not comparin' myself with anybody. My big hope is for a season when I get to play in every game. It hasn't happened yet. I feel great, and I hope this is the

175

year comin' up. When I get to bat, all I want to do is swing at that ball. I don't stand there making comparisons."

"You're being too modest, Mickey."

"Modest, heck!" Mickey grinned. "You guys don't know it, but it's tough enough to make a showing against all those great pitchers and teams I gotta face. The way you fellas are comparing me with stars like Ruth, Foxx and Gehrig, why I got a long way to go before I can even think about things like that. Besides we got ourselves a pennant to win. I don't have time to think about those things."

But the argument was on among fans everywhere.

Would Mantle ever hit sixty home runs? Some said he would. Others hooted the idea. But their eyes were all on Mickey. Not since his rookie year at Phoenix in 1951 had Mickey's spring-training exploits resulted in so much publicity.

The spotlight was on him, and the longer it stayed on the tougher he got.

There were new faces that Casey Stengel brought up for the 1956 season. Tony Kubek, a youngster from Milwaukee. Norm Siebern, Marv Throneberry and Bobby Richardson all looked like future Yankee stars. Casey's big problem was Phil Rizzuto at shortstop. Phil had been the star, the bulwark of the Yankee infield for fifteen years, now he was thirty-eight years of age and he was no longer the spark plug of the great champions. But all of Casey's problems seemed to vanish into thin air when Mantle started his assault on the great Ruth's record of sixty homers.

Three days after his tremendous opening-day blasts against the Washington Senators, Mickey poled out homers three and four against the Tigers. Then in rapid succession he blasted two homers in Boston and three in Kansas City. In Cleveland, hitting against the league's top hurlers, Early Wynn and Bob Lemon, Mickey drove out his tenth, eleventh and twelfth circuit blasts.

Nothing is duller than mere dates. But when practically each day sees a new homer the fans start counting and listing dates.

By the end of May, as just about every fan in the country knew, Mickey had already hit twenty home runs.

Would Mickey Mantle hit sixty home runs? Would he keep up the terrific pace and beat the great Ruth's home-run record?

The subject was no longer one for mere idle talk. Mickey was actually ahead of Ruth's record as May ended. By May 31, in the famous year of 1927, the Babe had hit only sixteen homers.

In previous years there were other super-great stars who challenged the great Bambino's record, and they came mighty close. Hank Greenberg of the Tigers, Jimmy Foxx of the Athletics, and Chicago's fabulous home-run slugger Hack Wilson all challenged the Babe's record, but in that final, big closing drive in September all three of the great sluggers fell short. Mickey? Well, maybe he would turn the trick.

Ted Williams went on record as saying that he thought Mickey had a chance to make it. "The way I see it," said Ted, "he's improving every year. This is the year he should get up there. There's no reason why he shouldn't hit .340. And he's the only guy who has a chance to break Babe Ruth's record."

As the red-hot summer wore on, that old injury jinx slowed Mickey down, but within a few days he was in there swinging from either side of the plate and taking dead aim at the home-run record. As the pennant fight raced into August, Mickey had driven out thirty-nine home runs, and according to the records he was just three weeks ahead of Ruth's mark. Ruth had not reached his thirty-ninth homer until August 20. Now fans jammed the ball parks to watch Mickey blast the ball. They came early to see him hit in batting practice, and they cheered him every time he lofted a drive into the stands.

The rival ball clubs were trying everything to stop Mantle and the thundering Yankee herd. Manager Lou Boudreau of the Kansas City Athletics even tried out a new defensive maneuver to stop Mantle. The strategy consisted of playing left fielder Gus Zernial back of the shortstop. Harry Simpson, the A's center fielder, moved over to left. Third baseman Hector Lopez moved over to short center field. Boudreau had hoped that this defensive alignment would halt the slugging Yankee stars, but when Mickey noted the strategy he conferred briefly with Stengel.

"If he pulls that stuff on me, I'm gonna drop the ball into all those unprotected spots. The heck with homers. A bunt is as good as a long one out there today."

"Good idea," said Casey. "Let's show this bunch that we can play it close to the vest. C'mon now, let's show those boys some smart playin'."

The count was 3 and 2 on Mickey in the third when, batting left-handed, he pushed a bunt to deep short. Zernial raced frantically for it, but Mickey easily outran the peg to first.

Nevertheless, the K.C. team wasn't sent back to its regular positions. So, when Mickey came up again he dropped another bunt single along the third-base line. By this time Boudreau and his team were through with the maneuver, and the Mantle shift was packed away in mothballs.

"Nothin' works against him," the fans said happily. "He'll hit 'em in the stands for you, over the fence, or, when you're waiting for a blast, he'll drop a bunt and run like Jesse Owens." But the thing that excited the entire baseball world most was his great home-run hitting spree. By June 11, he was eighteen games ahead of Ruth!

The most amazing thing, though, was that the fans were solidly behind Mantle. Even the fans of the Yankees' bitterest rivals, Chicago, Kansas City and Cleveland, were applauding every new Mantle drive.

In Detroit, for example, he slammed two home runs in a night game against the Tigers. Both of them were powerful blows that dropped the ball into the upper tier. Were Detroit fans enraged? They cheered him! The spectators were so taken by Mantle, and so anxious to shake his hand, that they jumped onto the field from all directions, and the game had to be halted while the spectators were cleared from the field.

There was bedlam on the field. The park police and ground crew couldn't handle the crowd. They all demanded to meet Mickey!

One reporter covering the game wrote: "Frank Sinatra at his height never had his fans in an uproar like that."

A telegrapher named Schonberger, who had spent forty years in the park sending the reporters' wires, said: "I've seen a lot of famous ballplayers play the game in Briggs Stadium, but never did I see any demonstration like the one today over Mantle."

"You know, Mickey," Casey said, as Mickey continued socking the ball, "lots of people comin' to see you play these days."

Actually, Mickey had developed overnight into the greatest individual drawing card in baseball, a player with such "personal draw" that fans were coming to see him slam the ball over the fence in batting practice. It got the players too, for when Mickey stepped into the batting cage during hitting practice, all work on the field halted and all eyes were on Mantle in the cage.

By June 20, Mickey had slammed twenty-seven home runs and was now eighteen games ahead of the Babe's pace in Ruth's record-making season.

And then on July 4 the old injury jinx again struck Mickey. He reached for a ball that suddenly took a funny bounce, and he had to twist to get it.

"And that," as he told the trainer working on him, "was when I felt the leg turn under me."

Mickey, in the midst of a race with Babe Ruth's record, was temporarily on the bench! With a lead over the Babe's pace of eighteen games, he had to sit around and watch the games fly by!

It was a disheartened and dejected Mickey Mantle who took the two o'clock train from Boston to see Dr. Sidney Gaynor, the Yankee physician, in New York. "It's the same knee I twisted fielding in the 1951 World Series," he told the press before he left.

"How long will Mickey be out?"

That was the question thrown at the Yankee staff after Mickey's examination. "It doesn't look too serious," answered Gus Mauch, the Yankee trainer, "but it's a day-to-day proposition."

Could Mickey get back in time to catch up with Ruth's record? Every day counted. To match the Babe's record had been something that no ballplayer had been able to do while playing in every game. Was it possible to do it while missing games? And would Mickey be able to play as well when he got back on the field?

These were questions that every fan was asking.

21.

"HI, MICKEY! Great to see you back!"

"It's great to be back. Let me tell you that!"

"Think you'll get into the game with the Senators?" the reporter asked.

"I sure hope so," Mickey said.

It was July 7 when he rejoined the team in Washington. He wore a brace on his right knee.

"I'll be ready, Skipper, in a day or two," he reported to Stengel.

"No, you ain't," answered Casey. "For the next few days you're gonna sit nice and quiet. I gotta see that you're ready for the second half of the pennant race. Might use you as a pinch hitter for a while. But now you just sit there and relax, sonny."

But there was no holding Mantle. He reported for the All-Star game and announced to Casey that he wanted to play.

The Mickey Mantle who strolled out to the field wore a single-hinge brace on the outside of the knee. It moved like a nutcracker, and it was about as welcome to a fast runner as a lead weight would have been.

But all Mickey cared about was playing ball again, and he would have played with braces on both knees.

"Let's see that ball!" he yelled to Warren Spahn, who was pitching for the Nationals in the sixth inning. Spahn, one of the great pitchers in the league, looked at Mickey, slowly pumped his arm and fired his fast ball down the middle.

When it came, Mickey drove the ball four hundred feet into the center-field seats for a tremendous home run. The fans rocked the huge stadium with their cheers. This was what they had come to see, and now they were happy.

The day was a great one for Mickey, but it was bad for American League fans, as the National League stars pounded out their sixth win in seven years.

But fans all over the nation cheered with Casey over Mickey's homer. Knee brace or not, Mickey could still slam homers. Maybe, in spite of the days he'd lost, and others he might lose because of the knee—well, maybe he could still catch up with Ruth!

So the clamor began again. "Will Mantle sock sixty homers this year?"

MANTLE HITS NO. 34. Mickey's home-run tally became part of the headlines telling how the Yankees had fared the day before. In paper after paper, throughout the country, fans noted the daily count and checked with the calendar to see how many games Mickey had left.

MANTLE RAMS NO. 37. This was against Frank Lary of the Tigers. The blow was a tremendous smash against the façade above the upper deck in the right-field stands.

Mickey's thirty-ninth was against the Senators. Hal Griggs was the victim this time, and Mickey's wallop was one of his longest. The date was August 10, and he was eleven games ahead of Ruth, with forty-seven games to go.

On August 14, Mrs. Babe Ruth showed up at the Yankee Stadium to see the Yanks play the Red Sox. Actually, of course, she came to see Mickey Mantle in action. And he didn't disappoint her. He hit his forty-second homer that night. He was now thirteen games ahead of Ruth's pace.

"What do *you* think, Mickey? I've heard what everybody else thinks. Do *you* think you can make it?" This query from sportswriter Al Buck.

The question was beginning to get Mickey down. "All I'm tryin' to do is play ball," Mickey said. "That's all any player can try and do."

"Well, Mickey, however this season ends, you've given the fans a real treat for their money. It'll be a long time before anyone forgets the 1956 race. You've given baseball fans of the nation plenty to talk about for a long time." Mickey said nothing. He was feeling the pressure, but he tried to keep calm. He wasn't making any public statements. Instead, he kept hitting the ball.

On September 1, Mickey was paid a tremendous compliment. The President of the United States came to see him play against the Senators. This was no official visit, such as the one all Presidents make when they throw out the opening ball. President Eisenhower showed up, in a surprise appearance, to see Mantle play. He told James C. Hagerty, his press secretary, that he wanted to see Mantle add to his string of homers.

One little problem facing the President amused fans. Which team would he root for? Most fans knew that Ike was a Senators fan. But he was coming to see Mantle. Which team?

The President solved the problem neatly when he shook Mickey's hand while the press cameras clicked. "I hope you hit a homer, Mickey, but I hope Washington wins."

Mickey came through for the President. He smashed number forty-seven in that game.

And then the tremendous pressure he had been under began to get to Mickey. On September 1, he was four games ahead of Ruth. But the Babe's best pace had been at the end of the season. He had blasted the ball like crazy in that last month. Could Mickey, who had lost precious days because of his leg, actually keep smashing homers in the way he had been doing? He was far from being in first-rate physical condition. The leg was still bothering him and could conk out any minute.

As September rolled by, it became clear to Mickey, and soon enough to the fans, that he couldn't maintain the superhuman pace.

When the season ended, he had slammed fifty-two home runs! Only eight fewer than Ruth had in 1927! He had given it everything he had, and he had come mighty close to the greatest slugging record in base-ball.

He was the eighth man in baseball to hit more than fifty home runs in one season, and he was the second Yankee to ever pass the fifty-homer mark. Babe Ruth and Mickey Mantle were now the only Yankee players to pass the fifty mark.

And that was only one of the honors he had taken that season. In fact, he had swept just about every title. He won the league's batting crown with a .353 average. He batted in 130 runs. And he was named by the Baseball Writers Association, in a rare unanimous choice, as the American League's Most Valuable Player.

In the Associated Press poll of broadcasters and sportswriters, he was named as the outstanding athlete of the year in any sport. He received almost twice as many votes as his nearest rival.

Will Harridge, president of the American League, said that he had always ranked Babe Ruth and Bob Feller as the two standout attractions in baseball—the greatest crowd drawers. But now, he said, he had to add the name of Mickey Mantle.

"The reaction this office has received to Mantle's homers—distance homers—is positively stunning. I can't recall anything like it. Everywhere I went, it was Mantle, Mantle, Mantle."

He pointed out that when the Yankees came to town, the fans said, "Mickey is in town." "Mind you, they said Mantle first and the Yankees second. That's what they used to say when Ruth and Feller were in their prime." Beaming, he added, "I'm sure glad Mickey Mantle is in the American League."

Mickey had behind him a season that neither he, nor the fans, would ever forget. And he was only twenty-four years old.

22.

THE sun came out early and hot. Tom Johnson, head groundkeeper of the Yankee Stadium, sat in his underground office and previewed his schedule for the day. He was studying a sheaf of papers when the phone rang.

"Johnson talking."

"You'd better get out to the field," the caller said. "There's a guy wandering around out there. It looks fishy, so I thought I'd let you know."

"Thanks," Johnson said, quickly putting the phone down. There had been some peculiar things happening around the Stadium grounds lately, and he wanted to see what was going on.

He got up and hurried out to the field. Shading his eyes against the strong sun, he could see a figure in a business suit near the center-field wall. Trotting briskly, Johnson made his way across the field.

"Hey, you!" he yelled when he came near the man. "What're you doing! Better get off the field before I phone for the police!"

The man turned and Johnson could see that it was Mickey Mantle.

"Why, Mickey!" he said. "What're you doing here so early? You and the rest of the payers don't get here until about ten-thirty. It's only nine now."

"Hi, Tom. I was just lookin' over these plaques and readin' what it says on them."

Mickey didn't have to point to the plaques. Johnson, the whole Yankee team, and every Yankee fan knew about those plaques. There were three of them, celebrating three of the greatest figures in baseball history—all famous Yankees.

One plaque honored Babe Ruth, the greatest player of them all. Another told of the feats of "Iron Man" Lou Gehrig, the famed Yank star. The third was for Miller Huggins, the brainy manager of the Yank team in the Ruth era.

"You know, Tom," Mickey said, "there are times when it's all like a dream. I wake up in the middle of the night and I pinch myself. I say to myself, 'Mickey, did this all really happen to you? Are you really a Yankee?' Then I get down here early, to prove to myself that it's all really true."

"It ain't hard to see how you feel," Johnson said.

"I've just been standin' here and readin' what it says up there about these great men. They, and a few more like them, were tops. You know, I read now and again in the paper how this one and that says I'm up there with those greats." Mickey nodded his head. "Not me, Tom. I'm just thrilled every time I put on that uniform and get out there to play."

Johnson had seen a lot of players. Some he liked a lot, and some not so much. There were all kinds among players, just as among people in general. But he'd always liked Mantle. And this morning he felt fonder of the young player than ever before.

"I've been standin' here thinkin' of all the people who helped me make my way," Mickey said. "My dad, Mutt. I can't tell how much I miss him. I think about him every game I play. And Gramps, the best grandpa a fella ever had. Casey—well, everybody knows he's like a second pa to me, the best friend I got. And there was Barney Barnett, and Tom Greenwade, and so many others. Heck, without them I'd probably still be workin' in the mines."

Johnson just listened. He knew what Mickey was trying to say. Johnson knew, as did the whole Yankee staff, the amazing story of the rise of the poor miner's son to a top place on a top team.

"And when I think that now Casey's got me battin' in the cleanup position in the '58 season—that's Joe DiMaggio's old spot—well, you can't blame me for wonderin' if I'm dreamin'."

Then Mickey started walking toward the clubhouse and Johnson walked along with him.

In the dressing room, Mickey peeled off his jacket. "I might as well try on my new uniform," he said. "I hope it's good and roomy."

Then, after he had it on, he said, "Tom, how's it look?"

Johnson stared at Mickey with an expert eye. Then he smiled. "On you the Yankee uniform looks great. It *fits!*"